Greene County

Virginia

Greene County

Virginia

A BRIEF HISTORY

Donald D. Covey

THE
History
PRESS

Published by The History Press
Charleston, SC 29403
www.historypress.net

Cover art: Blue Ridge Mountains by Diane Velasco.

All images are courtesy of the author unless otherwise noted.

First published 2007

ISBN 9781540229182

Library of Congress Cataloging-in-Publication Data

Covey, Donald D.
Greene County, Virginia : a brief history / Donald D. Covey.
p. cm.
Includes bibliographical references.
ISBN-13: 9781540229182
1. Greene County (Va.)--History. I. Title.
F232.G8C685 2007
975.5'375--dc22
2007027253

CONTENTS

Contents

PREFACE

Before a historical society was formed in Greene County there was a movement in that direction: a widow wanted the memory of her husband supported by information about the county; a teacher had information gathered throughout many years; a lady who worked with the mountaineers wanted them represented properly. In addition there were people who moved into the county who had an interest in its past. The local paper, the *Record*, was quite willing to use the writings of several of these people.

The Greene County Historical Society was formed in 1978. By any measure it is still a young organization. From its inception there were almost immediate problems with finding a meeting place. A fire in 1979 destroyed the county clerk's building and did considerable damage to the adjacent county courthouse. For this reason court was held in the second floor of the old jail. Temporarily, the building now used by the County Health Department was available. Later the Greene County Board of Supervisors allowed the society to use the second floor of the old jail, and there was an understanding that the organization would be allowed to use the first floor when it became available. The small group moved ahead printing the *Greene County Magazine* and collecting items of historical value for a museum, confident that they would soon be able to use the first floor. As it turned out, use of the first floor of the old jail was not available until 2006. The society moved, but not always forward. The group continued publishing the magazine and collected a reasonable number of items for the museum, but by the middle of the 1990s there was some doubt about whether the organization would continue.

In 1994–5 there was a change in the Greene County Historical Society. There was really no question of the society giving up, but there seems to have been weariness among the members. As a result of various changes, within a year or two that weariness dissipated. Some members who had not been able to participate in society activities found that they now had time to be active again. New members joined and took part in society events. Many activities continued as before but with renewed energy. Publishing of the *Greene County Magazine* continued, but the magazine soon took on a different, larger format. Monthly meetings continued with the hope of attracting new members.

For several years the society helped by providing food for members of the Battle of Stanardsville reenactment. The society was not responsible for this activity, and when the owner of land where the "soldiers" bivouacked decided that the land could no longer be used, the effort was discontinued. A new member of the society had a great interest in the cemeteries of the county. The result of this interest was two books indexing the names of people buried in the graveyards of Greene County. Another member had for some time collected marriage records from the foundation of the county to 1900. The result was another book. The society, in an effort to reach new people, found room at the County Fair to talk with people, to tell them about their families and possibly to sell books. For several years there was a Strawberry Festival in Stanardsville in which the society took an active role. In addition, the society was largely responsible for a Fourth of July gathering. On one occasion the parade included all the candidates for sheriff.

Members of the society played a prominent role in the effort to find and record historic homes in the county, and were behind the successful effort to have Stanardsville declared a historic area. During this time, the society continued to actively seek the use of the first floor of the old jail—unsuccessfully.

The Greene County Historical Society entered into a third period of its existence when, in the 2004–5 edition of its newsletter, it was able to announce that the county administrator had told members that they might have the first floor of the old jail. This possibility occurred because of a ruling that the County Voters Registration Office must move to a larger area than what was available in the old jail. It was in 2006 that the office was finally available and the society could begin work. The first efforts involved making the building useful as the museum. After opening a doorway from the main entrance into the first floor, the society made various repairs to the old building. This included carpentry work for shelving, making duct enclosures, improving ceiling tile work and lighting and renovation to the bathroom. The next step was the addition of smoke, fire and burglar alarms. A museum must also have a climate control system (air conditioning and humidity control). Of course the purchase of appropriate furniture for a library was also necessary. The next step was to raise money to pay for all of this work.

Seeking a grant, the Society went to NiSource Charitable Foundation of which Columbia Gas is the parent company. Columbia Gas has been in Greene County for a number of years. The society requested $19,000—an amount that they were a bit surprised to receive. Other rather large gifts have been helpful as well. One member of the society offered $1,000, and challenged ten other people to make similar contributions. On a somewhat smaller level the society has been given at least two very necessary computers.

The society has begun to ask for volunteers who will be able to spend several hours in the museum when it opens. They were undoubtedly a bit surprised that two people from the University of Virginia Library offered advice in the proper storage and conservation of the various categories of artifacts that the museum will have.

The society has not been exclusively concerned with the museum. Publishing of the *Greene County Magazine* continues. A third volume of cemetery records is in production. The original person involved in this work unfortunately died a couple of years ago, but others have continued the work. At the time of this writing, 245 farm gravesites have been found and thirty-one mission, church and town cemeteries have been recorded.

Though it was not an original project of the society, a number of the members were active in the successful effort to establish the Stanardsville Historic Area. A related program is led by a member of the society. A collection of pictures of old barns and sheds throughout the county will be available long after those buildings are simply history.

Acknowledgements

I lived in Greene County for twenty-three years, and as a "comer" I might have expected to be greeted with suspicion when I asked for help in understanding the history of the county. This did not happen. Rather, people were often quite willing—even eager—to help. When I write about a church, a store or community, in many cases I have found and talked with someone who has lived there or known about it. I cannot name all of the people who helped me. I should mention Woodie Parrott who, if he was not so deeply involved in the genealogy of his family, might have been the one to write a history of the county. My wife, Vivian, has been a wonderfully helpful editor and a very patient wife. To all of those who have given much help I say, "Thank you."

To my knowledge Mr. John J. Morris, a local lawyer, collected the first history of Greene County.
Probably inspired by the Centennial Celebration of Greene County (1938), he made numerous historical notes about the county. Unfortunately his notes were never published and may be found only in the library at the University of Virginia.

A History of Greene County by T.E. Johnson is our first published history. That was nearly forty years ago, and if the development of the county continues at its present speed, another history will be needed much sooner.

Meanwhile the Greene County Historical Society has published a number of *Greene County Magazines*. It has also published such books as *Family Grave Yards of Greene County, VA* (Earl Estes) and *Marriage Records of Greene County 1838–1900* (Eugene Powell).

I wish to dedicate my effort to those brave souls who were the charter members of the Greene County Historical Society. So far as I can determine they started with nothing. Though they did not plan it, they made it possible for me to become president of the society for a period of several years. It was a time that I thoroughly enjoyed. The result was the writing of this book.

GREENE COUNTY—THE LAND

That part of the Virginia Colony now known as Greene County was a part of Spotsylvania County when it was formed in 1720. It was a part of Orange County when that county was separated from Spotsylvania in 1734. Finally in 1838 Greene County was separated from Orange County. The division began at Cave's Mill on the Rapidan River and went south to Albemarle County. To the north, the Rapidan and Conway Rivers join to form a boundary with Madison County. To the west, Greene County meets Rockingham County at the top of the Blue Ridge Mountains. Albemarle County forms the southern boundary. This is Greene County, extending only eighteen miles east to west along U.S. 33 (Spotswood Trail), with only seven smaller counties in the Old Dominion.

Geography has often determined history. This is true of Greene County. The Blue Ridge Mountains lie along the western boundary of the county, and as a result, fully one-half of the county can be considered mountainous. The mountains are responsible for a well-developed drainage system by means of a number of rivers, which flow through the hollows between the mountains in a generally southeastern direction. The Conway and South Rivers, lying north of U.S. 33, finally drain into the Rappahannock River. Waters in the Swift Run River, Roach River and Lynch River, which lie to the south of U.S. 33, finally drain into the James River.

The eastern half of the county is in the western Piedmont Region, and though scarcely mountainous, it is quite rolling. Because of the mountains and rolling terrain, travel has often been difficult. There are only two primary roads (U.S. 29 and U.S. 33). Other county roads are narrow and seldom straight. While the ground rarely freezes enough to have spring thaw affect roads as it does in the North, mountain roads at higher elevations are frequently made difficult in winter by freezing rain or snow, and low-lying roads are apt to be flooded when rain is heavy.

Geologists trace the history of the Blue Ridge in "Greene County" back to the Precambrian Period some 1,100 million years ago, and suggest that much of the rock from that period originated in a sea bottom. The metamorphic and igneous rocks, of which the Blue Ridge is largely composed, are the products of great heat and pressure, and indicate the strength of volcanic action and earthquakes that occurred in a number of geologic cycles. The mountains appear at times to have reached nearly a mile in height. These periods of uplift were followed by thousands of years during which erosion took place.

Almost one-half of the county is forested. Unfortunately human misuse and natural disaster, such as the chestnut blight and fires, have reduced the number of merchantable timber. Except for a recent rock quarry near Ruckersville, and a couple of aborted attempts to mine copper, there is no indication of significant value in mineral or rock resources. Drainage by means of mountain streams tends to occur sporadically and rapidly causes erosion, and as a result, fertility is not high. The extensive mountainous and rocky terrain also tends to limit the utility of the land. As might be expected, the ground water level varies with, and is affected by, the topography, but the water supply is generally good.

Located as it is one hundred miles or more from the Atlantic Ocean behind the Piedmont Mountains, the county is protected from normal ocean weather but not from so-called "Bermuda Highs," which sometimes produce extended periods of extreme heat throughout the area. Nor is it protected from those huge tropical hurricanes that sometimes wander inland. With the Blue Ridge on its western boundary and other ranges of mountains about fifty miles farther west, the county is protected from most of the severity of storms coming from the north and west. However, the county is not immune to "backdoor" weather from the south, and to some extent, the north. Most of the snow in this area is the result of large quantities of moisture coming up from the Gulf of Mexico and meeting cold temperatures. The amounts of snow can sometimes be devastating. A statistical chart is included in the Appendix.

Since it was not a county until 1838, the term "Greene County" in quotation marks will generally be used throughout this early history in place of the excessive use of "that part of Orange County which is now Greene County."

GREENE COUNTY TO 1750

Prehistoric Life in "Greene County"

At least ten thousand years ago Paleo-Indians used to gather at a site in the Shenandoah Valley, only fifty or sixty miles north of "Greene County." They gathered along Flint Run, now called Thunderbird, to renew their supply of spear points and other tools. The plentiful jasper at this site proved excellent for this purpose. The occasional gathering was also a time of social contact, for these were hunters who had no permanent home. Their only shelter consisted of animal hides, which they stretched over a few saplings. For years it was thought that they preferred the Shenandoah Valley for their hunting trips, but in recent years archeologists have discovered a similar site on the eastern side of the Blue Ridge near Culpeper, Virginia. This suggests that these early men were more numerous and widespread than they were originally thought to be. They hunted in small groups and used heavy spears with large spear points—now called Clovis points after the site where they were first found. This type of spear was necessary for the hunting of bison, caribou, elk and possibly mastodon. It is not surprising that artifacts from that time ten thousand years ago are rare and have never been found in "Greene County." However, it is inconceivable that some adventurous group, possibly at a time when animals were fewer and more difficult to find, did not find their way into "Greene County."

Historians, including anthropologists, are fond of naming periods of time as Paleo-Indian, Early Archaic, Middle Archaic, Late Archaic, Early Woodland, Middle Woodland or Late Woodland. If we are not careful, we may think of these periods as distinctly separate boxes of time and culture. In fact, there was surely a process of slow development over thousands of years. For instance, in Paleo-Indian times the glacier was only about two hundred miles north of the Thunderbird area and the mountains were above the timberline. As Virginia warmed, trees grew to cover the mountains and some produced nuts. Bushes grew and produced berries. The inhabitants changed. Some followed the glacier north, while some remained and were joined by a movement up from the south.

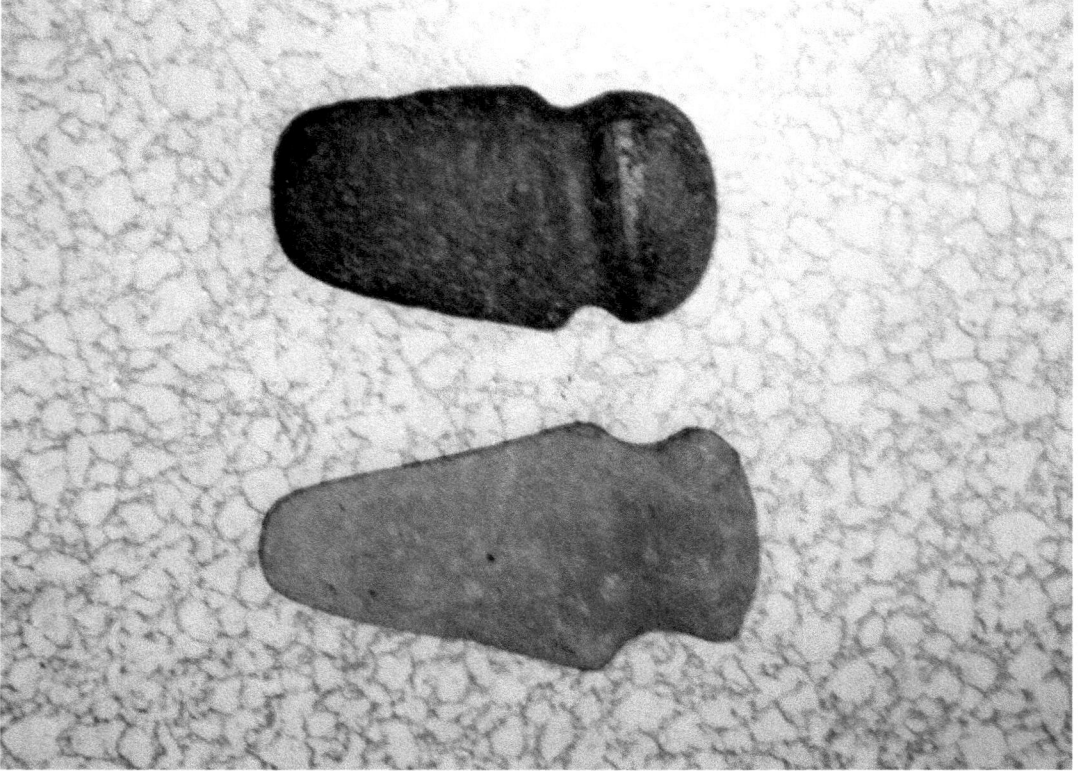

These stone axe heads may be seen in the Greene County Historical Museum.

About fifty years ago archeologists working in the Blue Ridge Mountains found and surveyed caves and rock shelters, and they found that these shelters were used over a considerable period of time. Somewhat permanent shelters made families and an increasing population possible.

Perhaps four thousand years ago stone axes were invented and this made possible the clearing of areas where edible plants might be encouraged. When they found that they could clear areas, inhabitants began to move down from the mountains. This does not mean that archaic men were farmers, but they could now take advantage of those plants that would grow in a lower part of the land. A number of axe heads have been found in Greene County.

Finding and eating nuts and seeds, the late archaic man faced the need to reduce them to a more edible state. The result was a simple hand mill with a shallow depression where grain could be crushed by a hand-held rock: the mortar and pestle! These devices could come in a variety of sizes and shapes. For instance, a pestle might be a simple round rock. These have also been found in Greene County.

There is evidence in Greene County of the use of rock shelters. One shelter was used twice during the Woodland Period. It was first used by Native Americans of the Piedmont area and later by Indians from the west of the Blue Ridge Mountains. It was probably used only as a hunting camp.

This small mortar and pestle were found near the Swift Run River by Dr. and Mrs. McClean who gave permission to use them.

This pottery vessel may be seen in the Greene County Historical Museum.

There came a need for cups, usually pottery vessels. If one needed to do more than roast, a "pan" was helpful. Most were so fragile that they are usually found in fragments, but Greene County is fortunate to have a whole vessel three-and-a-half inches in diameter and four-and-a-half inches in height.

The Monacan, probably the only Native Americans we can name as having lived in this area, may well have been influenced by the coastal Indians. They caught food from the rivers, and used the level flood plains along the rivers to plant and raise corn, squash and other edible plants. Other Native Americans called them *Siouan*, meaning "diggers in the dirt." They were indeed farmers, but the hundreds of small arrowheads that have been found in the county show us that they were still hunters. Through various periods the population grew. In early days the unit was a family, but as time went by the unit became a village. They lived together, worked together and buried their dead together.

Early explorers met the Monacan, but when early settlers arrived they found no Native Americans in the area. White man's diseases had taken their toll on native populations, and the pressure of white man's western movement probably caused those tribes that were left to abandon the land. Still, in Greene County there is a persistent belief that some residents in the hollows have some Native American blood. We do know that in the period between the earliest colonists and the arrival of settlers, traders and trappers found their way to the mountains. Historically, throughout the country traders took native women as consorts, but it is doubtful if there is any proof of Native American blood remaining in current residents.

Explorations

When Columbus sailed west in 1492, he was exploring in an effort to find another trade route to the East. Since he thought he had been successful in reaching India, he called the natives he found "Indians." Shortly after his voyage, England, France, Holland and Spain began exploring the edges of the new continent in search of a water route around or through to the East. It was the London Company—a trading company— that founded Jamestown. At the same time, believing that the Indian Ocean lay within reachable distance to the west, the colonists considered various means of getting across the land. They knew that there were mountains only about a hundred miles to the west. They probably learned this from the Native Americans, and certainly from trappers and traders.

A number of exploring trips were planned. They either failed to start, or failed to get very far. Finally Lieutenant Governor William Berkeley commissioned three exploratory trips by John Lederer. It is not clear what this twenty-six-year-old German scholar, who wrote in Latin and was a student of medicine, was doing in Virginia. Perhaps it was simply curiosity. His first trip is of great interest to us. On March 9, 1669, Lederer, along with three native guides, started west along the Pamunkey River, a short distance from what is now Richmond. Lederer wrote, "The fourteenth of March, from the top of an eminent hill [about twelve miles northeast of Charlottesville, Virginia, and a little less southwest of Gordonsville, Virginia] I descried the *Apalataean* [Blue Ridge] Mountains"

(Cumming 1958, 17). Subsequently he reached the *Apalatean* Mountains and climbed a high mountain where he mistakenly thought he could see the Atlantic Ocean. It took him four days to go sixty miles and reach his "eminent hill." It took another four days to travel the remaining thirty miles to the top of the Blue Ridge. Lederer's account of the trip and his map of the trip differ somewhat. However, if we accept that the map is more accurate than his words, he crossed the Rapidan River twice and continued westward until he came to a branch of the James River (today called the Swift Run River). If he then followed the branch up to the Blue Ridge, he must have climbed Hightop Mountain, 3,665 feet in height and located just south of the Swift Run Gap.

Sometime before 1973 Darwin Lambert, with three Native American guides, attempted to follow in the steps of John Lederer on his first trip. (In his account, Lambert gives friends who accompanied him the names of Lederer's "Indian" guides: Magtakunk, Hoppottoguch and Naunnugh.) He wrote, "We who were trying to follow think we found and climbed Lederer's 'eminent hill'...We studied the Blue Ridge as he had and chose the peak that looked highest [Hightop], though others are actually higher" (1989, 27). There is good reason to suppose that Lambert is correct, and that John Lederer, the first white man to actually report seeing the Blue Ridge, climbed Hightop Mountain and spent several days in "Greene County."

Lederer's reports on his trips were not well received. This reaction may have been the result of jealousy that a German should accomplish what no Englishman had been able to do. Lederer apparently had a better reception in Maryland, where he went thinking that he had been driven out of Virginia.

A new era in the history of Colonial Virginia began with the appointment of Colonel Alexander Spotswood as lieutenant governor of the colony. Spotswood was a member of an old and respected family in Scotland. He had become a colonel in the army, and fought—and was wounded—in the Battle of Blenheim. With this military background he had a different view of the need for exploring and crossing the mountains. The French were establishing outposts on the Great Lakes and on the Gulf of Mexico. The English must get over the mountains to prevent these French outposts from joining and surrounding the English coastal colonies. For all they knew about the inner geography of the continent, it might be possible to attack a nearby French outpost on Lake Erie.

John Fontaine was the only one to keep a diary of Spotswood's exploratory trip, which started out on August 29, 1716. Sixty-three men and seventy-four horses began the trip. It was an impressive group that included at least twelve gentlemen and their slaves, fourteen soldiers and four native guides. The trip across the Blue Ridge Mountains took eight days. The line of travel for the first three days is pretty clear, but for the remainder of the trip Fontaine's account leaves room for some debate as to where the group crossed the mountains. However, the preponderance of evidence indicates that they crossed at Swift Run Gap, having traveled for a couple of days in "Greene County." One simple but telling bit of evidence is Fontaine's account that they found the headwaters of the James (Swift Run) River, which flows east and "about a musket shot from this spring there is another which rises and runs down on the other side" (Alexander 1972, 105). Two centuries later these headwaters were still there. The men continued over the mountains where they proceeded to drink a toast (or two) to the King of England.

In the folklore of the county there is a story that Spotswood and his men camped by a lake about a quarter of a mile northwest of what is now the town of Stanardsville. The lure of this story resulted in a dance pavilion being built at the lake in the nineteenth century. There is no indication that the dance pavilion lasted for long, but the story continued well into the twentieth century. Another version of this story has residents of the area going to a spring where Spotswood had camped to get good cold water. This version continues to this day. While no writer who has studied the Fontaine diary has reached a similar conclusion, one is inclined to think that there may be a germ of truth in the stories, and that Spotswood did camp somewhere near the present site of Stanardsville, Virginia.

However, this expedition was headed for much rougher territory, and before they started, the horses needed to be fitted with horseshoes. This simple but unusual process apparently inspired Spotswood to give the men who accompanied him a remarkable memento at the end of the trip. We are told that he gave each of them a golden horseshoe in which colored stones represented the nails. On one side was the Latin motto "*Sic juvat transcendere montes,*" which means "How delightful it is to cross mountains." On the other side were the words, "The Tramontane Order." Unfortunately the golden horseshoes, if Spotswood did actually present them to the men, have all been lost. The incident is a mere footnote to the story of the trip, except in Greene County where the golden horseshoe has become its emblem.

Pioneer Settlers

John Lederer's expedition into "Greene County" had little real effect on the Virginia Colony, but the same cannot be said about Spotswood's 1716 expedition. Within twenty years almost all of "Greene County," excepting the more mountainous land, had been taken up in patents (grants) from the king of England—a total of about sixty thousand acres. It cannot have been coincidence that each night's camp was named for one of the gentlemen John Fontaine mentioned in his diary as members of Spotswood's expedition, nor that four of these gentlemen were surveyors. They were surely being encouraged to be entrepreneurs, land developers and land-grabbers. This they did with alacrity. There were certain requirements to be met in order for the recipient of a patent to keep his land. In general, within three years one must, depending on the type of land involved, "seat" and plant 3 acres, clear and drain 3 aces, raise 3 "neat" cattle or 6 sheep or goats, or build a building 20 by 16 feet for every 50 acres one hoped to keep. These conditions were not always met. For instance, the first eight men to take up the Octonia Grant on September 1722 did not meet the requirements and lost it. When it was finally awarded in September 1729, only one man, Robert Beverly, received the grant.

With regard to the Octonia Grant, when James Taylor Jr. made this survey he marked the northwest corner of the surveyed land on a huge boulder now known as the Octonia Stone. The mark was a figure eight with a cross above. Presumably, all the grants were surveyed and marked in some fashion, but this is the only mark to have been found. It remains the earliest physical evidence of the white man's presence in "Greene County."

This horseshoe emblem is used by Greene County.

The majority of men who received grants of land in "Greene County" from the king of England were wealthy, and they had no interest in occupying the land themselves. They would often place someone on the land to see that all the rules for keeping the land were met, or they would sell the land. We should look to those who did come to live on their land. These exceptions seem to be:

James Beazley
The first James Beazley settled on Saddleback Mountain in 1740. This is a little to the north of the present U.S. 33. In 1748 he purchased three hundred acres a short distance south of U.S. 33 and the Swift Run River, but still in the mountains. The name of James Beazley continued through at least four generations. It was James Beazley III who made a move into the eastern section of the county where he eventually owned about one thousand acres of land along the Swift Run River. One son was a farmer who

The Octonia Stone is simply a big boulder until one sees the surveyor's mark.

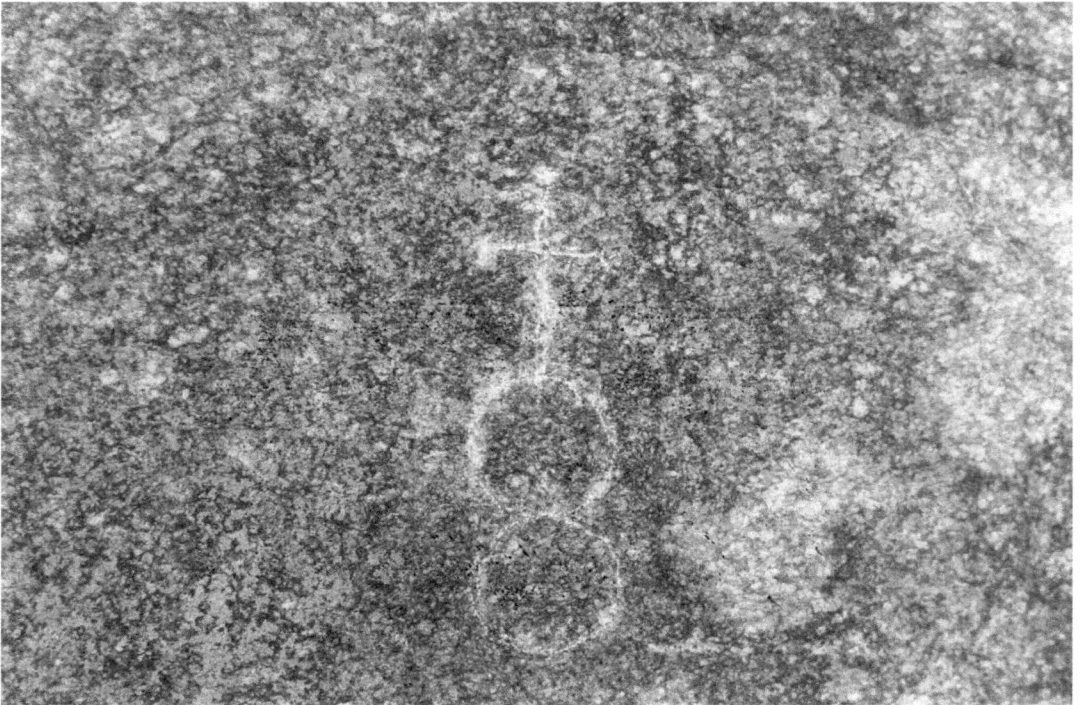

The surveyor's mark—a figure eight with a cross above—has no meaning in the present day. It probably had no religious meaning when it was formed and was simply a mark for the corner of the assured grant.

also owned a gristmill and a store. Another son was a doctor. A third son was a Greene County clerk, commonwealth attorney and finally a judge. The Beazley name is still found in Greene County with a slight change in spelling.

Samuel Estes

Samuel Estes had a grant of nine hundred acres in the southern part of "Greene County." Abraham Estes, possibly a brother, had a grant of five hundred acres, which he soon sold. However, it seems that the Estes family considered this their home, and early members of the family married into eight other families who probably lived nearby. The Estes name is still found in Greene County.

John Goodall

John Goodall bought eight hundred acres at the foot of Parker Mountain in 1749, and at a later date bought land up to the top of the mountain. At about this time he was appointed a constable in Orange County, which at that time included "Greene County," and was later appointed to the State Commission of Peace. By the middle of the nineteenth century the family was related by marriage to the Cox, Davis, Harvey, Huckstep, Ogg and Walker families.

Henry Kendall

Henry Kendall received a grant of four hundred acres in the South River area, and twenty years later he applied for his "headright" of fifty acres, which was given to men who had paid their own way to America. Henry had three children who married into local families, but the Kendall name is no longer found in Greene County.

John Mallory

John Mallory settled in the lower end of Bacon Hollow. Nathan, probably a grandson, was known to have provided beef for the soldiers during the Revolutionary War. A later family member, John, and his wife, Sarah, gave an acre of land to the trustees of the Bingham Methodist Church. This may have been where the present church was built.

William Monroe

William Monroe leased one hundred acres from George Taylor. There is no record of his having purchased land, but at this time leasing property was about the same as buying it. He must have prospered, for when he died he owned eleven slaves. William might have become simply another name on a list of early pioneers except for his remarkable will. In his will he made provision for a trust from which poor children in the county (Orange at that time) would be helped to get an education. This is remarkable for two reasons: William Monroe could neither read nor write, and impossible as it seems, remnants of that original fund still exist in Greene County and are still used for educational purposes today.

Honorius Powell Jr.

Honorius Powell, probably Honorius Jr., bought two hundred acres southwest of Stanardsville in 1739. The Powell family is difficult to trace, perhaps because this man had only daughters. However, the Powell family continues in Greene County to the present time, with members active in various civic organizations and efforts—including, at one time, membership on the County Board of Supervisors.

William Riddle Sr.

William Riddle Sr. leased one hundred acres of land in 1744. His son, William Jr., sold ninety acres of land on the south side of Swift Run River, so we know there was also an early purchase of land. The family is easily traced down to the middle of the nineteenth century because there was the repetition of the first names Fielding and Valentine in four or five generations. The Riddle name still continues in Greene County.

James Stodghill

James Stodghill moved to "Greene County" in 1732 and purchased two hundred acres of land lying on the Swift Run River. He continued to purchase or to receive land until he owned 1,200 acres, including a mill. His oldest son lived on the land until 1771. His youngest son, Joel, continued to live in the county until 1790. From that time, though a daughter is known to have married locally, the Stodghill name was lost to the county.

Thomas Walker

Thomas Walker received his "headright" in 1741 after receiving a patent of 340 acres just north of McMulllan, Virginia, and soon received a second patent of one hundred eight acres. His grandchildren were related to a number of "Greene County" families. The Walker name is still found in Greene County, but we cannot find a relationship to this early Walker family.

The Williams Family

The Williams family was in "Greene County" from its earliest days, and David Williams bought the one-thousand-acre patent from George Penn in 1730. In 1762, Edward, Francis and John Williams were ordered to provide workers for a western "Greene County" road. With the birth of Felix Williams, we can trace a consistent line down into the twentieth century. Williams is a common name, and it might be very difficult to connect those currently living in Greene County with this early family.

Early Roads in "Greene County"

Throughout Virginia, rivers and Native American trails were the first available means of transportation. When the hunters and traders ventured beyond the fall line of the rivers, they found the Monacan occupying the piedmont from the James River up to the northern areas of Virginia. However, by the time colonists actually moved into the territory the natives, who had previously occupied this territory, had either died or moved out, and it was their former trails that early white settlers of the area used for travel.

In the early days the word "road" had a much different meaning than it has today. In those days, several people may have been ordered to "view" a proposed roadway. If it seemed a reasonable route, a road would be ordered "cleared." This meant that at least a way to walk would be cleared.

The main crop, tobacco, required only a "rowling road" to get it to a river by means of hogsheads. Otherwise, land travel—mainly on horseback—generally used improved Native American trails, and since natives tended to live on bottomland along rivers, this is where early settlers' roads developed. Mountain gaps or passes were important in the Blue Ridge, and Native American trails tended toward rivers and/or mountain gaps. The Conway River forms a boundary with Madison County to the north. The natives surely lived and walked a path along this river, and we are not surprised that State Road 667 (Middle River Road) extends along this way. Although we cannot document the earliest use of a road here, it is reasonable to suppose that some sort of road was needed after Francis Conway and Anthony Thornton patented five thousand acres along the Conway River in 1732. It is interesting to note that the old Thornton House, built in the mid-1800s near the confluence of the Conway and South Rivers, faces north toward the remains of an old road along the Conway River, which was probably an extension of the road to the Conway Plantation.

A mile or two south, the South River flows down from the mountains eventually turning north into the Rapidan River. A native hunting camp near its banks is sufficient evidence that there was a trail along the river. Archaeological discoveries at this site indicate that it was occupied (probably seasonally) by several nearby groups of Native Americans, some of whom came from the western side of the Blue Ridge. The trail has long since been obscured by State Roads 621 and 637.

The Swift Run River flows down from the Swift Run Gap through Mutton Hollow, and is today closely followed by State Road 634. As it flows around the north side of Parker Mountain, Swift Run River is followed by State Road 624. It can be no accident that the James Beazley family, which originally made its home on Goose Pond Mountain just outside the eastern border of the Shenandoah National Park, found its way downstream to about one thousand acres of bottomland, and that part of State Road 624 is now called Beazley Road.

To the south of the county is the Roach River, originating near Powell Gap and flowing through Bacon Hollow. It is followed by State Road 627.

The Lynch River, which meanders along, uncertain whether it belongs to Albemarle or Greene County, is followed by State Road 628.

We can speculate that the Native Americans made a trail down and across several of these rivers as they hunted game, or visited other tribes. It is State Road 810 (Dyke Road) that winds along the foot of the Blue Ridge in a similar fashion.

Several roads that had nothing to do with rivers or Native Americans developed. In the early days, the heaviest traffic was undoubtedly on the mountain road from the Fredericksburg area. If you were in "Greene County" looking east, it was called the

Fredericksburg Road—State Road 609. What is now U.S. 33 developed rather early as a road from the central area of Virginia.

A couple of roads led eventually to Charlottesville. One of those was State Road 604, now known as Celt Road. The other was State Road 743, also known as Advance Mills Road.

3

GREENE COUNTY—1750 TO 1800

Topographically there are two Greene Counties: the western mountains and the eastern section. It is interesting to observe that there seem to have been two Greene Counties throughout most of its existence. The statement, "There's always been them and us," made by a person who could be identified with the mountains, expresses the feeling of many even today, and is verified by considerable historical fact.

Darwin Lambert states that, "Only after people from Europe and Africa had lived in these mountains for a century and a half [roughly 1700–1850], coming and going or staying a decade or several generations, did anyone consider mountain people here lastingly different from lowland people" (1989, 171).

This may be true. First, the earliest people to arrive were of English, Scotch, Irish or Welsh descent. These men, with names such as Beazley, Goodall, Kendall, Page and Powell, came in patenting or buying enough land to at least establish small plantations. They were accepted and given duties in what was then Orange County. In the early days they lived in houses similar to those throughout the county, their home life was similar and they raised tobacco as did most of Virginia. Second, no significant number of men seem to have gotten up into that part of the Blue Ridge Mountains now taken by the Shenandoah National Park, and considering the names of those who were brought down from the mountains when the Shenandoah National Park was developed, one-third had not even arrived before Greene County was established in 1838.

The early men who established plantations would have been raising tobacco, a crop which was terribly work intensive and which quickly depleted the soil. As a result some of these men moved over into the valley, while others moved down into the lower parts of the county. Those who remained faced increasingly difficult conditions. When people did begin to occupy the higher mountain areas, they were living on stony soil. Often animals could not be used on the rocky land, and cultivating had to be done solely by human labor. Farms were necessarily small. For most it was subsistence farming and living. Until well into the twentieth century travel throughout the county was difficult. It was far more difficult in the mountains, and so mountain folk were for all practical purposes isolated and dependent on their own resources for food, clothing

This mill appears to have been up in the mountains and was obviously very old when the picture was taken. *Provided by Emily McMullan Williams.*

and what social life they might have. The multiplicity of mills—flour mills, gristmills and saw-mills—is an excellent example of their successful effort to be independent.

James Stodghill, a pioneer settler, brought his wife and two children to "Greene County" in 1732, and bought land on the Swift Run River just west of Parker Mountain. His land included a mill on the river. Almost two hundred years later David Sturgill, interested in finding his roots, came to Greene County. He knew that his ancestors here had owned a mill, and he asked a native of the county to help him find at least the foundations of that mill. The native could not be of much help to David because he knew of five mills that had existed along that part of the river, any one of which might have belonged to his ancestor. That mill may have stayed in the family for a time. Others were passed from one owner to a purchaser. One can still find the remains of millraces and foundations of mills throughout the county. A number of old mills remain, silent for generations. We may know where some mills were and who owned them, but we will never know of all the mills that existed in the county.

In the early days, the men in the eastern section of the county did live pretty much like those in the western mountains. Then, in the second half of the eighteenth century, a number of men began to move in, and because the rolling land allowed, they were able to assemble large plantations. They also raised tobacco, but had room to develop new fields. The work was difficult, but rolling land allowed the use of animals for work that could not be done by slaves. A couple of real villages developed in their midst (Stanardsville and Ruckersville). Their culture developed in its own direction.

Since the history and culture of these two areas of Greene County went in different directions over a rather long period of time, it seems wise to consider them separately beginning in the second half of the eighteenth century. We should note that even within the eastern section of this very small county there were feelings of separateness. An elderly lady in the Ruckersville area showed her keepsakes to a visitor: antique dishes, saddlebags her postmaster father had used in delivering mail and a saber belonging to a Civil War ancestor. She expressed concern about what might happen to these keepsakes when she died, and the visitor suggested that some of them be given to the Greene County Historical Museum. She answered, "But that's in Stanardsville." Then she explained that her parents had such strong feelings on this issue that they had sent her to high school in Barboursville, Orange County, instead of Stanardsville. Later the same visitor learned of a considerably younger lady raised in Ruckersville whose parents had sent her to Charlottesville rather than to Stanardsville High School. However, these two villages are only six miles apart, and the topography and general history combine to override the differences. We do not consider these as two different areas.

The period from 1750 to 1800 contained three important events: the French and Indian War, the Revolutionary War and the founding of the United States.

The French and Indian War

The colonial lieutenant governor may have been concerned that the French and their Native American allies might surround the colonies and prevent them from expanding to the west. This could have been of little concern to the people in the Blue Ridge Mountains—they may have occasionally seen a half- or quarter-blood native, but the tribes were long gone and the French were nowhere near. However, several men served in the army—perhaps just to join the fight.

John and Richard Lamb both served. They probably were precursors of our present Lamb families, but we do not have the records to make the connection.

There was a James Riddle who served. He may have been the son of William Riddle, a Pioneer settler who leased or bought one hundred acres of land along the Swift Run River in 1744.

Thomas and Charles Walker served. Though Orange County had several Walker families, it seems quite likely that the pioneer settler, Thomas Walker, who patented 340 acres of land in "Greene County," was their father.

Perhaps several people helped the war effort in other ways. John Goodall, who served as an Orange County constable in 1749, was appointed to the State Commission of Peace in 1759, apparently as a reward for some special service in the war.

No part of the French and Indian War occurred in Orange County. While several men from the mountain section of "Greene County" served in the war, we cannot be sure anyone from the eastern part of the county did so. Since so few men in the county were directly involved in the war, and there were no engagements even nearby, it seems evident that those who lived in this area felt little threat from the Native Americans or the French, or were greatly affected by the war. Of course, we should remember that at this time the county was sparsely occupied.

The Revolutionary War

In the period from 1773 to 1776 Lieutenant Governor Dunsmore dissolved the House of Burgesses several times. At such times, its members, including Thomas Barbour and James Taylor of Orange County, held revolutionary conventions. This still included "Greene County." During this period counties set up Committees of Safety. Members of the Orange County Committee of Safety railed against Governor Dunsmore, whose troops had confiscated munitions that the committee felt belonged to the county. It published approval of various actions against the British, including those of the minutemen at Concord in 1775. Acting as a court, the committee considered certain pro-British pamphlets that were found in the county, and had them burned. Early in 1776 members of this committee took an oath "to be faithful and true to the Commonwealth of Virginia, and to the utmost of their power support, maintain and defend the Constitution thereof as settled by the General Convention" (Scott 1907). It was such feelings and actions throughout the colonies that brought revolution in the same year.

Probably a number of the men of the "Greene County" mountains had gone there to get away from the source of government. Already a long way from their county government, it seems unlikely that men felt greatly oppressed by the British, as did those along the coast, or even in the eastern part of Orange County. The Stamp Act and the Tea Tax would have affected them very little. They scarcely were acquainted with the writers of the day who were expressing principles of liberty. They, or their fathers, had left the British Isles for one reason or another, and had come to a new continent to get a new start. However, some mountain men joined the fight—probably simply hoping to rid themselves of the British and avoid paying taxes to support the English (Anglican) Church.

Men in the eastern part of "Greene County" were living nearer to the seat of Orange County, and may even have served as leaders in some militia. Often, they seem to have served as lieutenants or captains during the Revolutionary War.

The Colonies Become the United States

At the national level, the change of colonial rule from England to the formation of the United States was a traumatic experience for the leaders of all the former colonies. Each former colony must have had similar dramatically disturbing experiences, though much diminished from those at the national level. It is a fact that a number of the states (former colonies) felt independent. They often felt no allegiance to a neighboring state. Making a nation was difficult. However, considering all these problems is not our responsibility. In the counties, including Orange County, there seems to have been much less difficulty. Those holding county offices in the colony simply seem to have moved into similar positions in the state controlled county. Other changes came slowly enough that they caused little disruption in the lifestyle of the people.

4.

MEN OF THE WESTERN MOUNTAINS
OF GREENE COUNTY

These are some of the men and/or families primarily identified with the western mountains of "Greene County" during the period of 1750–1800. They are men who also served in the Revolutionary War in "Greene County," or elsewhere:

James Beazley Jr.

James Beazley Jr. returned after the Revolutionary War, and seems to have taken up the life of his father, James Beazley Sr. Both men were undoubtedly plantation owners who actively bought and sold land in the mountain area. If James Beazley Jr. ventured into the piedmont area in his trading, it is not immediately evident.

George Bingham

George Bingham, after serving in the Hanover County Militia, bought land in 1784 extending from the county line along Lynch River to the top of what has become known as Bingham Mountain. In 1791 he was granted a license to perform marriages in Orange County. According to a deed recorded in Albemarle County in 1796, Bingham was one of seven men who bought an acre of land, which lay across the county line into Orange County ("Greene County"). There they established the Bingham Methodist Church, which still exists today. A son, Joseph, remained in the county, marrying and eventually becoming a justice.

The Goodall Family

John Goodall, the pioneer, had three sons—John, Richard and William—who were lieutenants during the Revolutionary War. There was also a James Goodall, perhaps a grandson, who served in the Revolutionary War.

John and Richard Lamb

Both John and Richard Lamb, who served in the French and Indian War, again served in the Revolutionary War. It is unfortunate that we cannot connect them with the Lamb family of today.

John McMullan

John McMullan came from Dublin, Ireland, in 1760. He enlisted in the Continental Army in 1776. He moved to Georgia in 1787. McMullen spent a rather short time in "Greene County," but his descendants were so involved in the life of the county that their efforts can still be seen in the name of a community.

John Melone

John Melone served in the Revolutionary War while in Maryland. He came to "Greene County" in 1792, buying land in the mountain area. As the father of eleven children, he was the precursor of a large Melone family. That family produced two sheriffs of Greene County: John Wesley Melone (1880) and Russell (1940).

Reuben Roach

Reuben Roach served in the army after having purchased 175 acres of land southwest of Parker Mountain. Ten years later he purchased fifty acres east of the Roach River, near Roach Pass. This leaves us wondering if the river and the pass were named for him, or for an earlier member of the family. Deeds were sometimes lost or never recorded. Three other men from Orange County with the Roach name served in the Revolutionary War, but we cannot place them in "Greene County."

Ephraim Simmons Jr.

Ephraim Simmons Jr. arrived in "Greene County" in the late 1850s. After serving three terms in the Revolutionary War he, too, bought land, but he soon moved into Albemarle County. Simmons Gap is named for this family.

The Taylor Family

George, Erastmus and Zachary Taylor each patented one thousand acres of land in the first rush to get land in "Greene County." It is difficult—if not impossible—to connect these men with the present Taylor family in Greene County. We do know that another Zachariah Taylor applied for a pension as a Revolutionary War veteran.

Thomas Walker

Though there is certainly some confusion over the number of Thomas Walkers in the area, it appears that the same Thomas Walker who served in the French and Indian War also served in the Revolutionary War.

We know little about them and we may not have all their names, but there were others from the mountains who served in the war. Jonathon Cowherd, John Davis and James Haney are among those who served.

A number of men made contributions to the war effort in the form of large amounts of beef. Others helped by pasturing beef. Occasionally someone gave a musket, which was probably never returned. Some of these were "pioneer settlers": James Beazley, John Goodall, John Page, James Stodghill and John and Richard Lamb. There were second generation men who also helped: James Beazley Jr., Robert Golding, Thomas and Nathan Mallory, James and Lewis Riddle and Charles Walker.

5

Men of the Eastern Section of Greene County

The Revolutionary War was a different matter for the leaders in the eastern part of "Greene County." Some of these men came to the county before the Revolutionary War, and about as many came after. One company of the Orange County militia was used for guard duty at the prison barracks in Charlottesville. It was commanded in succession by Captain Jeremiah White, Captain Robert Miller and Captain May Burton Jr.—all of "Greene County." Others may have seen action at Yorktown.

Following are some of those men from the eastern section of "Greene County":

John Beadle

John Beadle was appointed lieutenant in the Orange County militia in 1780 and captain in 1787. He bought a total of over eight hundred acres northwest of Stanardsville, and built a two-story, log house with chimneys of English and Flemish bond at either end. The house stands today in the Greene Acres Subdivision.

Quite incidentally, he once owned two of the original lots in Stanardsville. One of those was where the Episcopalian Church now stands. Through the marriages of his children, he became related to eight other "Greene County" families.

James Beazley

In an effort to separate the various men named James Beazley, it may be helpful to consider them together. James Beazley I finally settled near Goose Pond Lake a short distance east of what is now the Shenandoah National Park. He did not take part in any war.

James Beazley II enlisted in the army during the Revolutionary War, and saw action in Brandywine, Germantown and Yorktown. He returned to "Greene County" and continued in his father's footsteps as a trader of land.

This log house was built by John Beadle in the late 1700s. *Permission to use picture given by present owners, Kenneth and Carol Weiss.*

James Beazley III, born in 1794, fought in the War of 1812. He had nearly one thousand acres of land near the Swift Run River, along what is now Celt Road. He owned a mill, a cooper's shop and a store. The Beazley family cemetery may still be found on property, which originally belonged to him. He was the first coroner of Greene County, and in 1842, was a justice of the peace. His three sons were James Beazley IV, a farmer, Robert Beazley, a doctor, and Wyatt Beazley, a county clerk, attorney and finally a judge.

May Burton Family

May Burton Sr. was born in the early 1720s. His grandson, May Burton Jr., was born in 1752. By one estimate they amassed a plantation of about three thousand acres. Their land lay on the south side of the Rapidan River and north of Ruckersville, where they built a tavern and a mill. A hamlet developed there for a time. May Burton Sr. was remembered as the lay reader in the Old Orange Anglican Church. May Burton Jr. reached the rank of captain when he served in the Barracks Prison in Charlottesville, Virginia, during the Revolutionary War.

Benjamin Burton was the owner of the Orange Mountain Mills (flour mill and sawmill), which may have been the first enterprise to encourage the development of Dawsonville, a hamlet several miles to the east.

A descendent, Dr. May Burton, owned a home on land just northwest of the original tavern, where it stood until recent years.

Isaac Davis Jr.

Isaac Davis Sr. was a sheriff of Albemarle County, and later served in the Virginia legislature. Isaac Davis Jr. served in the Albemarle County militia, and eventually became a captain. He moved to "Greene County" where he owned five hundred acres of land. In fact "Greene County" deeds credit him with the purchase of much more land. Looking to the west, he owned one hundred thousand acres of land in Kentucky. He served as a justice of the Orange County Court, and then as high sheriff there. In 1796 he began the construction of his home, Locust Grove, which remained in the family for six generations.

His son, Thomas Davis, was an attorney, and became a state senator from Orange County. Thomas is still remembered as being instrumental in the formation of Greene County.

Descendants of Isaac Davis Jr. have held these important positions in Greene County: sheriff, commonwealth attorney, Greene County treasurer, Greene County commissioner of revenue and county supervisor.

The James Early Family

James Early was born about 1750, and during his life, he owned over eight thousand acres of land in "Greene County." We should note that his father, John Early, was known to have purchased over twelve thousand acres of land in "Greene County." James was an ensign in Shackleford's company of the Orange County militia, and became a captain of the company in 1793. Earlysville, Albemarle County, was named for James Early Jr. His descendants who were engaged in public service include an attorney, a commonwealth attorney, a state senator, a judge and a deputy secretary of defense under President Truman. The Early family has owned a number of well-known homes in the county: Buffalo, Guilford Farm, Westover and Wakefield.

William Parrott

William Parrot served in the Northumberland County militia during the Revolutionary War. Moving to Orange County, he was appointed a justice of peace, and soon became the sheriff. When Greene County was formed in 1838, he was the first sheriff. In his days as sheriff, he was responsible for the collection of taxes and was bonded for $50,000. Unfortunately, two deputies stole all the tax money, and William Parrott lost a fortune in repaying the money. Fortunately, he was able to recoup his losses and retain his reputation. Members of the family still live in the county.

John Rucker

John Rucker was sent into "Greene County" to choose a site for a new Anglican Church. Members of the family owned large acres of land, and Ruckersville is named for them. It is said that members of the Rucker Family have served in every war in which the United States has been involved, though this cannot be proved by Greene County records. Two of John's sons patented the bateau, a boat widely used by tobacco growers along the James River to carry their product to Richmond. It is still used once a year as people enjoy a race along that river.

George Shearman

George Shearman first served during the Revolutionary War at the Barracks Prison in Charlottesville, Virginia. His final service was at Yorktown. A son, George Washington Shearman, was a justice of peace in Greene County. Another son, Thomas M. Shearman was a physician. A grandson, John Shearman Chapman, was both an attorney and a state senator.

William Stanard

William Stanard inherited six thousand acres of the Octonia Grant—all of which lay in "Greene County"—from Robert Beverly. He spent most of his life in Spotsylvania County where he was appointed a justice of the peace, sheriff and finally a member of the Virginia House of Delegates. He spent no more than five years in "Greene County," possibly to take his family away from the conflict of the Revolutionary War. During this time, he planned Stanard Ville, as he called it, and laid out ninety lots, many of which he sold. It became the town of Stanardsville. The state of Virginia declared it officially a town in 1794, and it became the county seat when Greene County was recognized as such.

George Stephens

George Stephens, the first of three with the same name, bought two hundred acres of land in "Greene County" in 1796. Deeds show that he purchased at least 1,400 acres through the years. The 1846 will of Robert Stephens Sr. is a good indication of the possessions in the family at that time. Robert Stephens Jr., after the death of his mother, was to get the homeplace and three hundred acres, the Burton farm, the Price farm and the Ollie Eddins farm. Children Tandy and Alton were to get "my quarter" and the Plunkett farms near Swift Run Baptist Church, the Samuel Scott Place, the Harlow House, the Old Store House and lot at Quinque and the New Store House. A son, George, was to get the mountain farm. There was also mention of a Texas Grapefruit Farm.

The White Family

The White family name is not to be ignored, but it is difficult to follow the family line. Jeremiah White was a corporal in the Revolutionary Army. John White served in the Orange County militia during the Revolution. Richard White was a lieutenant in the army. William White, son of Jeremiah, served as a lieutenant in the army, and became a major in the Orange County militia. He then became an attorney, and served his county as a magistrate, as a sheriff and as a collector of revenue.

The War of 1812

The War of 1812 inspired far less response from "Greene County" residents than any other war. Men who we know served in the war were James Beazley III, Robert Holbert and Granville Kennedy. They may have seen action at Hampton, and at the protection of Washington, D.C. Both efforts were unsuccessful. All three must have been strong Methodists, for two joined in giving land for the Mount Paran Methodist Church and the third gave land for the Mount Vernon Methodist Church.

6.

"Greene County" and the Decline of Virginia

Virginius Dabney, a recognized historian of Virginia, considered the first half of the nineteenth century a period of decline in Virginia. By 1850 nearly 382,000 citizens of Virginia had moved—often out of the state—and Virginia lost many men of leadership quality. They left because fields in the older parts of the state had become exhausted by overuse in the raising of tobacco. There was also overuse of fields for the raising of other crops. It was easier to go west or south to relatively empty areas where soil was rich. In addition, land in the west was cheap land.

A considerable number of men urged the adopting of known means of improving agricultural methods, but a greater number of men seem to have had a mind-set against new methods of improving the fertility of the land. These methods seemed expensive. On the other hand, shipping tobacco to Great Britain was no longer as profitable as it had been. Slave labor seemed an easier way to go than expensive methods. But slave labor was inefficient.

It was often men of some wealth and with leadership ability who moved. Without good leadership, men accepted poor leaders who generally tended to continue thinking in the past.

"Greene County," though small in size, seems to have been one of those areas to which some men moved. The movement began shortly after the Revolution. Men with some leadership ability, and the subsequent generations, became leaders in the county. They often established large plantations and became somewhat prosperous. However, it is not at all clear that they adopted good methods to conserve the fertility of the land. To a considerable extent, they depended on slave labor. In the census of 1804 there were 2,447 whites and 1,740 blacks in "Greene County." They did not bring prosperity to the county.

7.

THE FORMATION OF GREENE COUNTY

For the mountain folk of "Greene County" little changed as they moved into the early years of the nineteenth century. We can still see the basic house of that day. Sometimes it stands alone. At other times we may find that a larger house has been built around it. Sometimes, when a succeeding generation needed more room, they simply attached another, bigger house. The original house was a small, one- or two-room house, often built of logs and with a loft. It had a stone fireplace and chimney on one end. This "saltbox" type of house often had a roof that sloped down over a shed in the rear, giving it the name "catslide."

At one time the roads of Orange County were compared to bridle paths. Horseback was often the only means of travel. The mountain roads of "Greene County" cannot have been much different in the early days of the 1800s. The social events of this period were described as "log rollings, house warmings, sugar stirrings, quiltings, apple butter bilins, corn shuckings, house raisins, and the Old Virginia Reel" (Bean 1938, 41). These activities describe a small, closed-in community.

If we look to the eastern part of the county, by 1838 most of the men we have considered had long since made their mark. One had served as sheriff of Orange County, another as a justice of the peace. Most had served in the Revolutionary War, three or four as captain of a company of the Orange County militia. All had worked for the county in various ways.

The "Upper District" of Orange County (now Greene County) had a population of over four thousand. It was an area beginning to develop, but in many respects living conditions throughout the area were quite similar. The roads were almost impossible to use for six months of the year. It was forty miles from the mountains of the "Upper District" of Orange County to the courthouse. Getting there involved a two day trip to and from the courthouse, and the trip was costly in both time and money for food and overnight lodging.

In that part of Orange County, which is now Greene County, whites formed 60 percent of the population and blacks 40 percent. In the rest of Orange County those figures were reversed. There is the suggestion that in the "Upper District" there was a concern—perhaps even a fear—that the slave population might sometime outnumber the white population throughout the county.

Certainly there had been calls for separation from Orange County for some time. In 1792 Madison County was separated from Orange County. It seems likely that they had some of the same problems that now disturbed "Greene County." Soon a northwestern area of Orange County petitioned that it be annexed to Madison County. It is not surprising that in the early nineteenth century there were a number of petitions, pro and con, related to this problem of separation from Orange County. Residents of Orange County did not want to lose control of the only road, which led them to the Shenandoah Valley, and petitions continued to be sent to the assembly in 1819, 1821, 1823 and 1832.

The final effort to bring about the formation of Greene County fell to Thomas Davis. He was elected to the Virginia House of Delegates from Orange County in 1827. A year later the political wars in the county pitted Thomas Davis against James Barbour, former governor of the state, former United States senator and secretary of war. Davis won, and in 1838, as a senator, he presented a petition for separation of the "Upper District" from Orange County to the Virginia General Assembly. One hundred twenty-two citizens from all parts of the area had signed it. "An act forming a New County out of the County of Orange" passed and the county was named after Nathaniel Greene of Revolutionary War fame (Parrott 1979).

Stanardsville was chosen to be the county seat. It was, and still is, the only officially recognized village in the county. In 1835 Stanardsville had one hundred forty-two residents. There were five stores, two taverns, one tan yard, a saddler, one boot and shoe shop, a tailor, two blacksmiths, a wheelwright, one hatter, a gunsmith and a physician. It was ideally located on a main road near the center of the county. On January 25, 1838, a group of county leaders met and made a list of men recommended for the various county offices. The governor, accepting the recommendations, appointed sixteen justices. The eastern section of the county—and in particular Stanardsville—profited greatly from the creation of Greene County. Plans for the courthouse, jail and clerk's office began immediately.

This should have been an interesting time for the mountain folk. They must have looked expectantly at the possibility of having court meet much closer to home, and in fact a good many mountain people had signed the petition that went to the State Assembly. As it turned out, few—if any—of the sixteen justices of the court had any compelling concern with the mountain area. Except for the proximity of the court house, life went on as usual.

Petition

To the Honorable Legislature of Virginia

The petition of the subscribers, citizens of the upper end of Orange County, State of Virginia, most respectfully sheweth.

That your memorialists participating in common with their fellow citizens in the enjoyment of free government, have ever looked with interest to the prosperity of our republican institutions, as the best guarantee for security of the many and diversified blessings as a community of freemen. It is our great priviledge to enjoy under our happy Constitution, and none do we recognize with higher spirit of exultation than the right of petition to the constituted authorities of the country for the redress of our grievances, which right can only be withheld when we cease to be free, and which we have hitherto refrained from making known to your honourable body, in consideration of the political excitement of the public mind upon the subject of the reform of the State Constitution, by which modification we had some reason to hope of relief under the then contemplated remodeling the counties by a new organization of the Government.

Your memorialists further represent to your honourable body, that the great distance at which they reside from the seat of justice of their county, renders it both in convenient and expensive in attending court: being often detained there by serving on juries, being detained as witnesses, and the more frequent procrastination of law suits, and not unfrequently by the high water of two rivers that intersect their traveling thither or returning home, and the extreme badness of the public highways from beyond the mountains to the Court House, which is nearly impassable for six month of the year or during the winter season. Orange County is about seventy miles in length, and for some distance above the Court House. the breadth is but ten miles. It being thirty or forty miles from the Court House to the top of the Blue Ridge, which divides this county from Rockingham. The above obstacles and inconveniencies often prevent the magistrates from this part of the County from attending court, and the public business is thereby injuriously neglected. The great and many privations which your memorialists labour under, have induced them to ask your honorable body to enact a law authorizing a division of the county of Orange by a line running nearly north and south from some point in the Albemarle line between Cavesville and Barboursville to the head waters of Marsh run, thence with the meanderings of the mouth of said run, emptying into the Raped Ann River, the dividing line between Orange and Madison. This division would form a compact county tending from the said designated line to the top of the Blue Ridge, a distance varying from twenty miles, embracing a population of about seven thousand industrious citizens, many of whom, by their daily labour, are subjugating the huge mountains to all the valuable purposes of agriculture. Within this boundary a Court House may be located at Stanardsville, which is near the center, & the citizens, like most of the other counties, will be enabled to attend court and return home the same day, which they can seldom do in their present condition. Stanardsville is situated 23 miles from Orange Court House, 25 from Charlottesville, 34 from Harrisonburg, and 15 from Madison Court House. By the location of a seat of justice there, the citizens (a greater proportion of whom reside above there) and the magistrates would be enabled to attend court promptly and dispatch the public business without delay. Wherefore, by this division of the county, no injury whatever can arise to the remainder of its citizens, and while we rely on their magnanimity in the spirit of equal laws for a hearty co-operation in behalf of our sovereign rights, and a redress of our grievances we look with confidence toy our honourable body, the legislature of our State, to grant this petition of your memorialists which they deem reasonable and worthy of your deliberate consideration.

Wm C. Jennings

Hazlewoth Riddle

Durret Oliver

James Lamb, Junior

Abram Eddins

John W. Taylor

Hiram S. Eddins

Bluford Eddins

Wm Riddle

Fielding Riddle

Parks Goodall

Thornton Rogers

James Burus

St. Clair Williams

Wm Eaton

Augustine Gear

Nathaniel Gear

Matthew Knight

Wm Dunivan

Thomas Slaton

John Gear

James Gear

Michael Mayers

Daniel Runkle

John Hanes

Wm Nichols

Tandy Sims

Smith Eddins

James Lamb, Senior

William Lamb

Wm Powell

George Shearman

John Marr

Levi Morris

Zachariah Taylor

Henry Warren

Bezaliel Parrott

Madison Marr

James Beazley

Y.L. Garth

Hugh R. Powell

Wade H. Snow

Jonathon Price

Granville Kennedy

William Shiflet.

Slaton Shiflet

Joseph Morris

Eliot M. Burton

S.L. Goodal

Thomas J. Eddins

James Follett, Sen

Hiram Marsh

Robert Dean

James Follet, Jun

St. Clair Dean

Peter Marsh

George Thornton

Addison R. Booten

Gabriel Powell

Edwin Nichols

Layton F. Eddins

Absalom Morris

Daniel Bert

John Small

Armstead Long

John Lamb, Jun

Samuel Harris

Elijah Huffman

Henry Fleck

Enoch Simons

John Shiflet

Emanuel Runkle

William Dean

James Ancel

George Powell

Downing Smith

Tazwell Marr

Cornelius Dean

John Haney, Senr

Wyat Snow

John Fleck

Wm Houseworth Poplar Run

John Higdon

William Willcocks

Jackson T. Powell

Mordecai Buckner

Thomas M. Shearman

Fielding Powell
James Warren
William H. Simms
Simon Powell
Charles Parrott
William Rogers
John M. Sims
Robert B. Winslow
Wm Sampson
Joseph Jarell
Ransom Lamb
Albert Eaton
Stewart Marks
Thomas Tyler
May Haney
John Haney, Junr
Davis Shiflet
Wm W. Parrott
Noah Smith
Abraham Taylor
Wm C. Knight
James Haney, Junr
Matthew Lamb Junr

Sanford Dean

John H. Melone
Achiles Rogers

Jacob Fleak
George Dean
Sanford Dean

8.

THE CIVIL WAR

In the Civil War the only significant action in the Blue Ridge Mountains of Greene County occurred in March 1862 during the famed "Stonewall" Jackson campaign in the Shenandoah Valley. Jackson had been told of a band of deserters up in the mountains, and had sent Captain Harry Gilmor to rout them out. There was thought to be a group of two to five hundred men under the leadership of a man named Gillespie in one or more hollows not far from Swift Run Gap. Gilmor had twenty members of his own company, and a company of militia infantrymen with which to rout them out. Perhaps it was the strangeness of the territory that discouraged his men. At any rate, after two or three days of fruitless effort to dislodge the deserters, Gilmor took his men back to Jackson and reported the difficulties. At that point Jackson sent two companies under Captain Lyn B. McMullan of Greene County and Captain Naderbush to break up the band of malcontents who were holed up in Hensley Hollow. They drove the deserters out and over the mountains into Greene County where they captured them, forty-eight in number. No explanation for the disparity between the number of men supposed to have been hiding in Henley Hollow and the number actually captured has been found, but this minor incident during the war must have provided considerable excitement for the mountain people.

There is a story that "Stonewall" Jackson used the Golden Horseshoe House, now located on the south side of U.S. 33 at the eastern entrance of the Shenandoah National Park, for his headquarters. While it seems possible that Jackson may have had reason to make a short stop there, it seems unlikely that he would have had a headquarters on the east side of the Blue Ridge while his troops were fighting on the west side.

In April 1862 General Richard W. Ewell received directions from General "Stonewall" Jackson to move his division from Brandy Station into Greene County to protect the road across Swift Run Gap. This would also place him in a better position to join Jackson over in the Shenandoah Valley. The 8,500 soldiers in two camps were more than the entire population of Greene County. During the short period they were camped in eastern Greene County some of Ewell's men contracted an unknown disease (probably typhoid fever). The sick were treated in the basement of the Stanardsville Methodist Church, in the Lafayette Hotel and in other available buildings by local women who served as nurses, but in spite of all efforts over thirty men died. They were buried somewhere near the Shiloh Baptist Church in the eastern end of the town, but it is no longer possible to find the exact gravesites. However, late in April the movement of all those soldiers through the county and over the mountains must have been quite an experience for residents.

In 1864 the Union armies planned and carried out a diversionary drive through Greene County to Charlottesville where they hoped to disrupt communications, destroy bridges and mills and generally divert Confederate attention from action at Richmond. General George Custer was in charge of 1,500 soldiers. On March 1, 1864, they stopped at Stanardsville long enough to destroy the Confederate Supply Depot there, search all public buildings and take the men of Stanardsville hostage during the raid. Custer's troops met a small Confederate force at Rio Hill near Charlottesville, and then began to retreat. During the retreat, Union and Confederate troops were in sporadic contact. As Union forces were trying to cross the Rapidan River from Greene County to Madison County there was a skirmish, now called the Battle of Stanardsville. Custer continued his retreat, having accomplished his mission.

The letters of Captain Francis M. McMullan and his wife, Jennie,[1] may give us a feeling for what problems the county experienced during the Civil War. Jennie sent her husband flour, jelly, sugar, fresh butter, clothing, paper, envelopes and apple brandy. She complained about the quality of the cotton and dyes she could obtain for making his clothes, and thought the leather available for the making of shoes was poor. We may wonder at the number of items Jennie sent to Francis, but early in 1864 counties were called upon to furnish meal, corn and meat.

There was a continued need for more men in the war effort. In 1862 Jennie reported that seventy-five males (colored) were required of Greene County for work on fortifications around Richmond. As early as November, Jennie reports that recently "conscript officers" arrested four men and shot and killed one who tried to run away. In August 1863 she reports that many deserters were passing through the western part of Virginia.

Inflation was extreme. At one time it was possible for a man to hire a substitute for his service in the army for $3,000. By the end of the war the cost had risen to $5,000. In January 1864 Francis expresses concern that Confederate currency and bonds may never be redeemed. Later he reports that $750,000 in bank money is now worth three million dollars in the new issue.

In the middle of 1863, after wounded men were brought into Stanardsville from battle, Jennie reports that people in Stanardsville were despondent—they had given up. In early 1864 Francis reports that discipline was terrible in Kemper's Brigade and that there might be extensive desertion. Eastern Greene County suffered when AWOL soldiers and Union sympathizers, hidden along the mountains, came down to raid for food and clothing. Finally the state assembly made it possible for counties along the mountains to set up patrols to deal with the problem. On August 10, 1864, the Court

---

1. Letters now owned by Emily McMullen Williams.

of Greene County chose forty men to do this. In September 1864 the court had second thoughts. They now named sixty men with a commander and three lieutenants, giving them instruction to arrest deserters and control the Negroes. We are left to wonder if two groups were necessary.

In January 1865 the governor issued a request or order to all counties to send one-tenth of all male slaves to work on public defenses around Richmond. The Greene County Court, knowing that the county had already sent 40 percent of its slaves to work in Richmond, simply refused to do more.

How did Greene County fare during the Civil War? From an incomplete list included in *Hardesty's Historical and Geographical Encyclopedia* (1884), of ninety-four men who served in the Confederate Army, seven were killed, eleven died during the war (probably from disease or wounds suffered in battle), thirty were wounded and fourteen others were captured. Of this group, two-thirds were casualties. There is no reason to believe that Greene County fared any better.

9.

Greene County Following the Civil War

During the Civil War no state saw more battles or physical destruction than Virginia. In addition to the ruin of vast areas of its land, Virginia suffered greatly from the loss of manpower. One hundred seventy thousand of Virginia's young men served in the Confederate Army. Fifteen thousand were killed, many more were left crippled by wounds and still more suffered from what was once called "shell-shock," but is now recognized as a psychological illness (post traumatic stress disorder or PTSD). Destruction in towns and cities was great, and the infrastructure was devastated. Many of those who might have been expected to lead the South out of its depression had been killed or wounded. The United States Congress was anything but helpful.

The rest of the century was an unsettling time in Virginia. While railroads expanded and several ports developed positively, most of Virginia—particularly farming areas—was in deep depression. As a farming community, Greene County could not escape the statewide condition. The mountain people could not have been entirely immune to this economic condition, but given the mountaineer's experience of living on comparatively little and supporting life by independent effort, he probably maintained his previous standard of living into the end of the century.

One man described the home in which his older brothers and sisters were born at the turn of the twentieth century:

> This house was built of logs. The chinks or spaces between the logs were daubed with mud. There were four rooms, two rooms making up the main part of the house, one upstairs and one downstairs and two sheds with earthen floors. There was a fireplace which burned pieces of wood three feet long or more. It was the only source of heat. The roof was covered with boards about three feet long instead of shingles (Knight, 13-14).

We could probably describe the house as accurately, though more critically, as a one-room house with a loft and two sheds attached. This house was not typical of all the houses in the mountains. In fact, this family does seem to have been one of the leading families of the area. They soon constructed more adequate quarters. It has been said that "while mountaineers did sometimes inhabit shoddy or dilapidated dwellings, most

We quote Senannie Beaty, the lady with the cane. Her house shows no signs of suffering from the Civil War.

were solidly-built wood-framed or hewn-log structures" (Haney 1996, 3). Nevertheless, this house was typical of a good many in the hollows and the mountains of Greene County at that time, and this type of house is about what we could expect to find erected about one hundred years earlier.

Likewise, the community events were described as "funerals, making apple butter, husking bees, making molasses, barn raising" (Knight, 66-127). They were similar to the description of such activities we saw one hundred years earlier. The standard of living and cultural events seem to have varied little for well over a century.

The eastern part of Greene County saw little physical damage during the war. Perhaps two or three mills, only one or two bridges and a munitions depot were destroyed. However, as many as two-thirds of Greene County soldiers were casualties.

This Victorian house built near the turn of the century shows no signs of suffering from the Civil War. *Picture by Ed Johnson. Permission from Allan Pyles.*

Along with the rest of Virginia, Greene County slaves were freed, and without slaves it was difficult—if not impossible—to maintain large plantations. Black people could no longer be compelled to do work and so became unreliable workers. Confederate money had no more value in Greene County than in the rest of the state. Bankruptcy was not uncommon, and plantations were sometimes broken up by sales to provide survival income. Surely the feeling of helplessness that gripped the state was felt in Greene County.

Though many blacks probably stayed near the plantation where they had been slaves, others formed little communities. Three are still known: Brush on the north side of Stanardsville, Scuffle Town or Gibbs Town about three miles southeast of Stanardsville and New Town on the eastern edge of the county and just north of U.S. 33.

During the nineteenth century Virginia held several constitutional conventions that made gradual changes to its government. While the Underwood Convention of 1867 and 1868 was not without its serious controversies, it did produce some landmark results. It ratified the fourteenth and fifteenth amendments of the U.S. Constitution, protecting the rights of former slaves. This was a necessary action to give Virginia a place in the Union. It also established free public schooling throughout the state.

Near the end of the nineteenth century as the Victorian period began, at least a few families were starting to recover. Senannie Beaty, who was of the right age to know, named a number of families who, at the turn of the century, were able to send their children to private schools. In the small village of Stanardsville there remain at least five excellent Victorian houses from this general period. There can be little question about the depth of the depression in the eastern part of Greene County, but apparently there was some recovery late in the century. It was also during this period that a number of country stores and hamlets began to appear throughout the county. This may have been another indication that the depression was coming to an end.

10.

MOUNTAIN FOLK AND THE CHURCH

The Methodist Church

The Methodist Church seems to have been the first denomination to appear in the mountains. As we observed previously, George Bingham came to the region in 1791 after having previously bought land on the south side of what is now Bingham's Mountain. He was also licensed to marry by Orange County in 1791. In 1794 Bingham, along with a number of trustees, purchased an acre of land from Harry and Sally Austin. The church, which they built on the north side of the Lynch River, was originally called "Austin's Meeting House." Later it became known as "Bingham's Meeting House." A church still stands there today, straddling the Albemarle-Greene County line. The preacher stands in Albemarle County and the congregation is seated in Greene County. At times the church has struggled. It was twice closed during the 1950s because of low membership, but because of its historic value it has come to life again and again as Greene County's oldest church.

In 1846 the South River Methodist Church was built on about an acre of land on the north side of State Road 637, about a mile east of the village of McMullan. There is some reason to believe that there was a group of Methodist worshipers around this village before the church was established, probably under the leadership of the Reverend Jeremiah McMullen.

Subject to repeated flood damage from the South River, the church was torn down and rebuilt farther from the river, probably around 1902. The church stands today as a successful rural church that has served the community well through the years.

In 1859 Downing Smith donated land on the south side of Spotswood Trail (U.S. 33), and about half a mile west of Lydia "for the purpose of erecting thereon a church" (*Greene County Deed Book* 1859, 769). The church was called Temple Hill Methodist. It continued until 1938 when it was sold to the Mennonite Missionary Board. It was abandoned by the Mennonites in recent times, and has since burned.

The Mount Vernon Methodist Church was built in 1861 on land donated by Granville Kennedy, who can be remembered as having served in the War of 1812. Harry Kennon, who continues to preach in Virginia and is now preaching in the

First United Methodist Church in Charlottesville, Virginia, tells us that there is strong evidence indicating that preaching services were held some years earlier in an old schoolhouse, which previously occupied the site. The first sermon preached in the new church was given by the previously mentioned Reverend Jeremiah McMullen. Today it is a successful rural church that has seen a number of additions and improvements through the years.

If one looks at the series of Methodist churches extending along the mountains from the South River Church, past Mount Vernon Methodist and Bingham's Methodist Church and down to Mount Moriah Methodist Church near Crozet in Albemarle County—all of which have long histories—one becomes convinced that they must have been served by a number of circuit riding ministers. Writing about the South River Church, Kennon says, "There is a persistent local tradition that the first American bishop (Methodist), Francis Asbury, spoke in the vicinity of the South River Methodist Church on one of his many sojourns through the area" (1992, 71). There is no corroborating evidence, but in any event these churches were fortunate to have local ministers such as Bingham and McMullen to build on the circuit riders' efforts.

Circuit riders and those who continued their work were simply carrying the word of God wherever people needed it and would listen. There is no evidence that in their early days these churches saw the mountain folk as a distinct group with special needs. The people who established these churches were local people who undoubtedly looked after needy neighbors, but did not see them as a different class.

The Episcopal Church

The Episcopal Church became interested in the mountain people of the Blue Ridge through the missionary concern of Frederick William Neve. Neve was born in England on December 8, 1855, educated in Merton College, Oxford University and ordained in the Church of England in May 1880. Thwarted in his desire to go to Africa as a missionary, he accepted a call and became the rector of the St. Paul's and Emmanuel Church in Ivy, Virginia. He must have found his work with the church members so slight that he needed to look for a greater challenge. He looked into the Blue Ridge Mountains, and came to consider them part of his parish. In fact, his work was so great and important there that on May 20, 1904, he was made archdeacon of the Blue Ridge.

Two concepts of the mountaineer grew up in the later half of the nineteenth century and extended into the early part of the twentieth. One romanticized the southern mountaineer as a pure Anglo-Saxon ancestor. Their songs, manners of speech and techniques of hand craftsmanship were recorded, prized and imitated by many who saw them as the remnants of an Anglo-Saxon agrarian past. It was in 1927 and 1929 that Rose and Paul Meadows and Alva and Bela Lam recorded fourteen songs for Okeh Records of New York and Richmond. In general these songs shared the shaped-note style, which began in the early 1800s. The University of Virginia has a two-volume collection of folk songs transcribed in 1935 and '36. Z.B. Lam, Polly Morris and H.B. Shiflett—all of whom could be identified with the western part of the county—contributed at least seventeen folk songs to that collection.

The other concept saw the mountaineer as culturally and spiritually backwards, and in need of domestic and religious training. In the period from 1890 to 1912 Neve started twenty missions, ten of which were in Greene County. As will be seen, the missions included chapels, schools, clinics or hospitals and "clothing bureaus."

Neve opened his first school in Greene County at Simmons Gap. He had advertised for men workers, but only women answered his ad. It was a woman who became the school's first teacher. The school, which was originally named St. Paul's School, with the addition of a chapel and cement block school became Holy Innocents School. It included a clothing bureau.

By 1903 a school was built on Wyatt's Mountain. It became known as St. David's School, and was eventually taken over by the Blue Ridge Industrial School.

About the same time Mission Home was built. It was a place where teachers came for rest and a renewal of spirit. St. Hilda's School was built, and the original cabin became a clothing bureau. The mountain folk became suspicious that the clothing may have been taken from dead people, and for a time there was difficulty. The successful response to this problem was the charging of a small amount for the clothing, which had previously been free gifts.

In 1905 a school/chapel was built in Pocosan Hollow toward the north. The building became a sort of community center for people who had a reputation for being difficult and sometimes lawless.

Again about the same time, a school was built on Hightop Mountain, the mountain where John Lederer probably looked west to see what is now Shenandoah Valley. For some reason this school had continuing difficulties until, in 1922, help came from the public schools.

In 1906 the St. James Mission was established at the foot of the mountains on the south side of U.S. 33. This mission soon grew to include "Jewel" chapel, a hospital, a school and a mission home.

In 1909 the Lower Pocosan Mission, down the mountain from Pocosan and closer to Stanardsville, was started. Here were a house, barn, clothing bureau, henhouse, ram house, milk house, chapel and school.

By 1910 "Cecil" Memorial School was started about two miles east of the St. James Mission.

A stone chapel was built. It is being used at this time by another church group.

Seeing the need to give the children advanced training beyond what the mission schools could offer, Neve set about establishing the Blue Ridge Industrial School. It took about three years to buy land in Bacon Hollow, build the necessary buildings and put together a staff. In 1910 a boarding school was opened where students could get a high school education, the first accredited high school in Greene County. There was practical training for future life in a rural area where the boys would likely become farmers and the girls, farmers' wives. However, in the middle of the last century

This stone chapel was part of the "Cecil" Mission by faculty and students. *Permission for the use of picture given by the school.*

the Industrial School had great difficulties, and even closed for a year or two in the mid-1950s. It probably was just not prepared for the changing times after World War II. Currently it is again doing very well as a school for boys who are not living and doing schoolwork up to their potential.

In 1912 Neve purchased a lot in the Haneytown area. Since there was already a school on an adjacent lot, apparently this mission did not develop as some of the other missions.

In 1915 the final school was opened at the urging of a Mr. Roche. It was known as Roche's Mountain School. There seems to have been no chapel, but the teacher, Caroline Makely, probably used the schoolhouse for that purpose since she did teach Sunday school.

As they watched the development of the Shenandoah National Park, Neve's missions struggled to survive. The park actually took over the property of only two missions—Simmons Gap and Upper Pocosan—but it moved the mountain folk out of their homes, and out of the mountains away from the missions. By 1940 all the missions, with the exception of the Blue Ridge School, had closed.

The chapel at the Blue Ridge Industrial School is being used by faculty and students. *Permission for the use of picture given by the school.*

The Brethren Church

As early as 1860 the Church of the Brethren began to come from the Shenandoah Valley over into Greene County. This was much earlier than the Episcopalians. By 1867 a Brethren family moved over into the county, and others followed. Ministers came over the mountains to hold services for these Brethren, and by 1896 the Evergreene Church of the Brethren was built. It is clear that the Brethren considered the Blue Ridge Mountains a mission field. Until the 1900s there is no weighty evidence that beyond their religious beliefs—including the wearing of plain clothing, the refraining from use of alcohol and tobacco and pacifism—they thought of their mission as anything other than the saving and nurturing of souls. Ministers came over the mountains from the Shenandoah Valley, preaching in various locations and staying for several months. In 1901 the Brethren organized five churches in Greene County into the Mount Carmel Congregation.

When Nellie Wampler and her sister, Ellen, came over the mountains to teach school in Bacon Hollow and minister to the people in 1909, there began to be definite evidence of social concern. The Brethren bought a farm in 1922 and built two large, three-story buildings to house the Church of the Brethren Industrial School, modeled to a considerable degree on the Blue Ridge Industrial School, which was already functioning. But by the 1930s state and federal governments became concerned about economic poverty in the area. Children were taken to school in Stanardsville by bus, and people living where the Shenandoah National Park was being established were relocated. In 1934 the Church of the Brethren Industrial School was closed. There was no more work to be done.

Baptist Churches

There are now probably more Baptist churches with more members in Greene County than those of any other denomination. A number of the Baptist churches belong to the Southern Baptist Association but probably several demonstrate their self-reliance by being known as Independent Baptists. One of those is in Bacon Hollow where a group of people gathered in what was originally a Church of the Brethren building. Though they are in theological agreement with other Baptist churches, they have never joined with the Southern Baptist Association.

The Liberty Baptist Church was formed in 1832. Originally their church building was across the Middle River from Kinderhook. There it was accessible to people from both Greene and Madison Counties. Because the building was nearly destroyed several time by overflows from Middle River, they eventually moved over into Greene County, about a mile south of Kinderhook.

This is one of the buildings of the Church of the Brethren Industrial School and dates back to c.1922. *Picture used with permission of Mike Skeens.*

The Mennonite Church

The Mennonites originated in the Anabaptist movement, which began in Switzerland in 1525. They were "re-baptizers," feeling that one should be baptized when he or she was converted and made the decision to join the church, not in infancy. Mennonites are fundamentalists whose most obvious doctrines are nonresistance and nonconformism, including plain dress, plain speech and refraining from any action, which might deter one from spiritual living.

Mission Home is in the far southwest corner of Greene County. It began in 1965 when the site was purchased from the Episcopal Church. It is a joint effort of the Amish Mennonite Aid and the Mission Interest Committees. Its work is to help mentally retarded children. Children come to the mission from a number of states, and without regard to religious or church background. The work of the mission is supported by a bakery, a broom-making shop, a woodworking shop and a small farm. Mission Home also includes a church that serves the surrounding neighborhood.

The Pentecostal Churches

The Pentecostal Movement began when a Brother Freed preached to the locals. Pentecostal churches are fundamentalist in belief. The first Pentecostal Holiness Church was built on Hightop Mountain very close to the Shenandoah National Park in the 1930s. Since they came into being at about the time the Episcopal and Brethren missions gave up their efforts in the mountains, one wonders if the Pentecostal movement took hold because the people felt the loss and a need for a church. The church on Hightop Mountain was difficult to reach—impossible in winter—and several churches have developed in places more accessible since that time.

11.

THE EASTERN SECTION OF GREENE COUNTY AND THE CHURCH

E xcept for the Anglican Church, which had its beginnings a century earlier, a number of denominations made their appearance in Greene County during the first half of the nineteenth century. Perhaps the first notable difference between the western area and the eastern areas of Greene County is the greater variety of denominations in the east. In addition, one must note the balance within denominations. There were eleven Episcopal missions or schools in the mountains. Only one Episcopal Church is located in the east. Similarly, though several Brethren churches remain in the west, there is only one in the east. There are many more Baptist Churches in the east, including black Baptist Churches. Part of these differences may be attributable to the greater number and variety of people who have moved into the eastern part of the county.

The Anglican Church

During the colonial days, the Anglican Church (Church of England) was undoubtedly the predominant church throughout Virginia. In 1725 the "Mountain Chapel" was built about a mile outside the northeast corner of what is now Greene County. It must have been a pretty shabby job because it soon needed replacing. In 1732 the bishop of Virginia sent two men, one of whom was John Rucker, to choose a site for the new church. They chose a site for "the Orange Church" about half a mile west of Ruckersville.

With the coming of the Revolution the unpopular Church of England could no longer exist, but it struggled to continue as the American Episcopal Church. In 1802 the Virginia legislature confiscated the glebe farms, the rent of which had been the church's means of income. It sounded a death toll for the Orange Church as an Episcopal house of worship. However, the building continued to exist as other religious groups began to worship there. At this time there is one Episcopal Church in the eastern part of Greene County. Grace Episcopal Church in Stanardsville celebrated its centennial in the year 2000.

The Methodist Church

At one time there were five Methodist churches in the eastern part of Greene County, but there is no indication that they were started or encouraged by circuit riders. Two of those no longer exist. Methodists worshiped in the old Union church—originally the old Anglican Orange Church—but Methodism did not thrive in the Ruckersville area. By about 1950 Methodists had moved away.

At the urging of Robert Holbert, a soldier in the War of 1812, Methodist services we held for some time in an arbor in the southern part of the county. Finally, with the help of Dr. John Early of Guilford Farm, the two men gave land for the Mount Paran Methodist Church. Unfortunately county churches are sometimes subject to deceasing membership. This happened at Mount Paran, and though the building still exists with a nearby cemetery, it has become a rather expensive home.

Today the most active of the churches is the Stanardsville United Methodist Church. It dates back to 1858. As an example of their activities beyond those devoted to religion, the church for years held a strawberry festival. It was so successful that it was taken over by the county for two or three years.

Of the remaining two churches, the Mountain View United Methodist exists because of an unfortunate division among the members of the Stanardsville United Methodist Church. However both churches continue to this day without any apparent discord.

The Westover United Methodist Church began when a group of Methodists started to meet in the school building of Senator Nathaniel Early. Today they continue to minister to the community in their own building.

The Baptist Church

There are six or seven Baptist Churches in the eastern part of Greene County, and one might suspect that there are more Baptists than any other denomination. The Ruckersville Baptists, who worshiped along with Methodists and Disciples of Christ, organized into a church in 1892 and soon built their own church building

The Swift Run Baptist church was organized in 1824 by a group of ten people. The church has not only survived, but apparently is flourishing. In recent times it has added several additions to accommodate the growing membership.

The Pleasant Grove Baptist Church is now in its second building. It celebrated its 170th birthday in 2000. In the building, one can still see the original gallery for slaves and much of the original church furniture.

The Stanardsville Baptist Church began as the Mountain View Baptist Church. When the Dundee Baptist Church closed its doors, many of its members had already moved closer to Stanardsville. With the purchase of land on Madison Road and salvageable parts of the Dundee Baptist Church, a new church building was constructed. Stanardsville Baptist Church was dedicated in November 1928.

The First Bible Baptist Church built its original building in 1971, and shortly after it was completely destroyed by fire. The congregation set to work and in two years rebuilt

The Bethany Baptist Church is one of two active black churches. *Permission to use picture given by the minister of Bethany Baptist Church.*

the church on the same site. By 1979 the congregation founded the United Christian Academy, which provides education from preschool through twelfth grade.

These churches seem to have been located where a group of people felt a need for a Baptist church.

The Methodists, and sometimes the Baptists, permitted people of color to sit in a balcony, but regardless of this fact there were at one time four black Baptist Churches. The Clerk's Book of the Liberty Baptist Church, a mountain church, records that in 1865 the church congregation allowed "colored folk" (probably their former slaves) to meet in the balcony for the purpose of organizing their own church. These freed men organized the Coram Baptist Church, which existed not far from the Liberty Baptist Church for some years. Gradually its members moved into other parts of the county. The church is no longer active.

Only a few people remember the Delovan Baptist Church. Two deeds convince us that the church did exist near the Collier Store in McMullan, Virginia.

Two other black Baptist churches still exist and are thriving to this day. The Shiloh Baptist Church is in Stanardsville, and the Bethany Baptist Church is located near the eastern border of the county.

Other Denominations

Several other denominations have in recent years appeared in the eastern part of Greene County. The Seventh Day Adventist Church has moved to larger quarters in Ruckersville. A Christian Church, at least until recently, rented space in the County Industrial Park. A Presbyterian Church has recently been started, apparently the first to exist in Greene County. Other evidence of the growing diversity among the people of Greene County, who for years were predominantly Baptist or Methodist, is the presence of a Roman Catholic Church, founded in 1980.

The local congregation of Jehovah's Witnesses might not appreciate being included in a discussion of Greene County churches, a term they never use. Nevertheless, they have their Kingdom Hall just west of Quinque.

12

THE MOUNTAIN STORES AND COMMUNITIES

In the later part of the nineteenth century a number of local men became aware that mountain people were no longer as independent as might have been thought. Increasingly, they needed everything from some types of food that they could not provide for themselves to shoes and nails. They needed better postal service and a place to trade such items as they had raised and/or harvested. These men set up stores around which there often developed some community life.

Fletcher Store

In modern terms all of the store owners were entrepreneurs, setting up a business by which they hoped to profit. Of these, John E. Fletcher may have been the biggest, if not the best. There is record that he may have had a store as early as 1859 when he was only twenty-two years old, and there are various records of store business from 1878. His daughter, Irma, carried on with the store until at least 1963.

The year 1879 found Fletcher making application to establish a post office six miles north of Stanardsville along the Middle (Conway) River. He was successful by 1884, and the post office continued until 1947.

He set up the Fletcher School and became the teacher. Fletcher was a farmer, and became the secretary of the Greene County Cooperating Grange. In 1893 he bought a mill, and we must presume that he also became a miller. However, his greatest interest seems to have been in the possibility of mining copper or other minerals in the area. Every effort seems to have resulted in disappointment. Finally in 1901 he received a letter telling him in rather strong language that mining was not feasible in this area, but he continued his efforts to sell or lease about two thousand acres for mining purposes. Fletcher died in 1906, and now various floods of the Conway River have destroyed or carried away most of what was Fletcher, Virginia. Only a house in which Irma lived, and a small building which may at one time have been the remains of the post office, can be found.

Kinderhook Store

In 1895 a Mr. Reuben Breeden purchased land several miles downstream from Fletcher, Virginia, and soon built a store. The Lamb Post Office had already been established there. Charles Dean purchased the store, and in 1908 the post office was renamed Kinderhook in honor of the hometown of President Millard Fillmore. A large house was built, and reminiscent of the earlier taverns and more recent rooming houses, salesmen who brought their wares often stayed overnight and ate the necessary meals there. The store served mountain people who brought dried cherries and apples, ginseng root, black walnut meats, eggs, chestnuts, rabbit, quail and oak tree bark to trade for needed products. If a customer needed change at the end of a transaction, he was given cardboard change called "due bills," which could only be used in the Kinderhook store. The store was the community center—a place to gossip, play card games or pitch horseshoes. A card game called "Set Back" is still remembered. Charles Dean was known to serve the living by pulling teeth, and the dead by acting as funeral director. A carpenter would assemble coffins in the upper floor of the store using hardware provided by the store. A horse drawn, glass-sided hearse was available for the funeral.

Collier Store

In 1842 Jeremiah McMullan, already an itinerant preacher, wrote in his diary:

> *This year I entered into the mercantile business with Rev. T.R.D. after one and a half years' trial I learned that this was not a profitable business. My pecuniary loss was much, but I learned much of human nature. I continued in the business for several years and then gave it up, finding it neither pleasant nor profitable* (Russell 1999, 10).

If he was keeping a store, it probably was in the house where he lived at the time, just about a hundred yards west of the present Scott Collier Store building. Though he was neither interested nor successful, he was one of the early McMullans to become involved in business. (We should note that the name McMullan was originally spelled with an "a," but at an indeterminate time later the family came to use an "e.")

It was not a store that started the development of the village of McMullen, but rather a gristmill. When James McMullen (1770–1842) turned from the raising of tobacco to wheat, it must have made the need for a mill obvious. This in itself would have attracted the attention of the neighbors, but through the years he added a sawmill, a cooper's shop and a carding machine. In addition, his son-in-law, Walter Houseworth, was a wagon maker. The mill and the surrounding activities became a place to meet, gossip and play. In 1846 the South River Methodist Church was established no more than a mile east of the mill. In 1854 Neal McMullen became postmaster of what was then known as McMullen Mill. When a store was built in 1886, it included the post office

The Collier Store with a post office known as McMullan, Virginia, was owned by Scott Collier for a number of years, and it was finally closed in the 1970s. It is still owned by the Collier family. *Permission to use picture from W.H. Collier.*

now known as McMullen, Virginia. The store passed through several hands until it was purchased by Scott Collier, who finally closed it in the 1970s.

Lydia Store

Lydia, Virginia, extended along U.S. 33 for about a mile and a quarter, from a store run by "Jack" Dean to a store run by Joseph Shifflett, on the edge of what is now the Shenandoah National Park. Lydia Post Office was established in 1896, but there was much more. A gasoline pump was added to the first store when automobile traffic became predominant. Up the mountain, behind the store, the Weaver family provided for a school until, in 1915, the Stanardsville School Trustees built the Lydia School about a mile above that first store. Across the road there was the Mountain View Tea Room, tourist cabins and even a dance hall. Down below, in the upper end of Mutton Hollow beside the Swift Run River, was "Jack" Dean's sassafras mill. Half a mile west was the Temple Hill Methodist Church. About a mile west was the Golden Horseshoe Restaurant and Motel. Somewhat behind the motel were the St. James Mission, school and hospital. Of course, a restaurant, motel, tearoom and cabins were designed for travelers along U.S. 33, but the rest of Lydia belonged to the mountain community.

The Tea Shop at Lydia, Virginia. *Permission to use this picture from Clinton Dean.*

Geer Store

In 1904 S.S. Geer started a store just north of the Mount Vernon Methodist Church on State Road 810. Here he also established a post office. In 1927 Mr. Geer sold the store to W.F. Morris who moved it just a few hundred feet farther north, and to the opposite side of the road. In those days he had one of those gasoline pumps in which the gasoline was pumped up from the underground tank by hand to a glass reservoir above the waiting car or truck, and drained down by gravity into the vehicle. Dried apples seem to have been the product of the mountains most often brought into this store for trade by the mountain people. As was common with these stores, the proprietor often made trips up into the mountains to serve customers who could not come down because of illness or storm. A baseball diamond was created and used in-season, but night after night through the year men gathered in the store just to talk. Probably because of the post office—though it no longer exists—the area is still called Geer.

Georgia's Store

Georgia's store was located in what became known as Haneytown, with All Saints Mission (Episcopal) at one end and the Church of the Brethren Industrial School near the other end. Rhoda Haney established a short-lived post office in this area, which apparently was responsible for the name Haneytown and Haneytown Road.

Shifflett Store

Several other stores were started farther south along State Road 810. The Shifflett Store was actually Georgia's store moved across the road from Mount Vernon Methodist Church. Its primary use seems to have been as a gas station.

Huckstep Store

Farther south was the Huckstep Store, which existed from 1908 until the 1940s. It was here that E.Y. Vernon, the community's funeral director, kept his supplies including a horse drawn hearse. Apparently, the store was successful.

March Store

Charles A. Pirkey started the March Store and post office only about two hundred yards south of the Huckstep Store. We don't know the real purpose for this store. Within several years Pirkey sold the store to Clarence Snow and Edward S. Morris. It was Morris who leased space to the Texaco Oil Company in 1930. E.Y. Vernon purchased this store in 1942, and probably moved his supplies here.

Pirkey Store

It is difficult—perhaps impossible—to get a clear picture of the stores and post offices in Bacon Hollow. Clyde Knight, who lived until recent years, recalled that his parents had a store in their home while he was still a young boy, and that later his mother became a postmistress. However, he wrote of an earlier store in the hollow. This may have been the Pirkey Store and post office, purchased and established by Charles A. Pirkey who at one time owned the March Store. Mrs. Knight, Clyde's mother, was postmistress at the Nimrod Post Office from 1919 to 1925. Bacon Hollow must have been a remarkable community. Aside from having probably the worst reputation in the county—it was an area in which men often produced alcoholic beverages without the needed permission of the state, and in the memory of many current residents, many Bacon Hollow men were known to hold back county and state police from their duties—at various times it possessed two stores (possibly more), two post offices, the Mountain Grove Chapel, Nimrod Shifflett's gristmill, a grade school and from 1910 the Blue Ridge Industrial School.

The Dyke Store dates back to about 1930. It was established by B.G. Snow. It continues today, run by a grandson. *Permission for use of the picture from Joel Snow.*

Dyke Store

In 1902 a post office was established about a half mile below the corner of State Road 810 and State Road 627, which ran down through Bacon Hollow. In 1921 B.G. Snow took over the post office and located it at his mill on the Roach River, which flows down through Bacon Hollow. By 1930 he moved to the intersection of the two roads. From that start Mr. Snow established a store, gasoline station and post office, which continue to this day. At the time Mr. Snow also ran a sawmill, and supplied much of the lumber needed to build the first building at the Blue Ridge Industrial School. In 1960 when the county elementary schools were consolidated into three, one was located in Dyke. Much earlier the Scourgeabout School was located near Dyke. We know only that Mrs. Snow taught there.

Herring Store

Early in 1912 Tom Herrring purchased five acres of land on the south side of Simmons Gap Road near the bottom of Shifflett Hollow. Here he established a store. The remains of his house and store may still be seen. Mr. Herring was also a blacksmith. He was known to take the role of dentist, at least in the pulling of teeth. He made coffins and conducted funerals. This was all typical of a mountain store owner in those days.

The United Dunkard and Bible Church stood about a mile and a half farther west, and beside it was the Shifflett Hollow School. Nothing remains of the church. A pile of broken lumber and metal marks the place where the school once stood.

Sullivan and Shifflett Stores

About another mile and a half farther west is the Manis Sullivan Mill where there was also a store. In this same time period Silas Shifflett set up a store farther west, where the Lynch River crosses the road. Some time after 1935 when these stores were no longer functioning, Mr. Snow brought goods from his Dyke store once a week to the abandoned school building for the convenience of local residents.

Events in the first half of the 1900s began to militate against the mountain stores. World War I undoubtedly took many of the young men out into other parts of the country, and often into Europe, where they could observe different cultures than the mountain culture to which they had grown accustomed. When they returned, they soon found that roads were improving as the state took over county roads in the 1920s, and cars were becoming available to ordinary people. In the 1930s the Shenandoah National Park created a most upsetting situation for many of the mountain people. Their way of living and their way of earning a livelihood changed. World War II came in 1942. Mountain stores could no longer supply the needs of these people, but Stanardsville, Charlottesville and even larger towns and cities were within reach on good roads. The day of the little mountain store was gone. Most of them existed for years, supplying a pack of cigarettes, a bottle of milk or a loaf of bread, but they could no longer compete with the larger stores available not far away. By some time in the 1970s all but one or two were closed. The store in Dyke remains the only one in business to this day. Its location on the major road into and out of southwest Greene County probably accounts for its survival.

13

Hamlets of the Eastern Section of Greene County

As we consider the mountain stores, they seem to have developed in a fairly logical order. For the most part they formed a sort of semicircle at the foot of the mountains and their community. More accurately, each store served its own little community, but those communities collectively comprised the mountain people. As we might expect, in the eastern part of the county there was logic to the development of every hamlet, but each came about in its own time and for its own reasons.

Burtonsville

May Burton Sr. and May Burton Jr. owned a large plantation of about three thousand acres along the Rapidan River and the Mountain Road. The building of a mill and a tavern were clearly obvious actions. At some point in the second half of the 1700s the hamlet of Burtonsville developed. There was a tavern, a mill, a store, a distillery, a blacksmith shop and a wheelwright shop. It was a gathering place for men who often played a game called "Five Battery." A fire insurance policy dated 1805 insured a building that contained living quarters, a retail store and a tavern on the plantation Pleasant Forest. The fire insurance policy indicates that the building had been previously insured. The entire building was seventy-two feet long, with store and tavern twenty-two feet deep and living quarters thirty feet deep. At that time they were valued at $1,100. At some time, possibly 1825, the building burned. The present building on the same site (the northeast corner of U.S. 29 and State Road 609) is said to have been built in 1826. We have no information about the decline of the hamlet.

Ruckersville

Thomas Rucker was the father of John Rucker II. This John Rucker purchased land on the north side of U.S. 33, and about a mile east of what is now U.S. 29. He built a log house there, which still exists within the structure of a much-improved home, and called it Friendly Acres. Sometime before his death in 1794 he named the area Ruckersville in honor of his uncle, John Rucker I. We have no reason to believe there was an actual village there. However, John Rucker II owned six hundred acres, and Peter, possibly a cousin, owned nearly eight hundred acres nearby. In those days a plantation had to have slaves who were trained to do all the equipment repair, building, etc. that were necessary. In effect, a plantation was a small, self-contained village. It is interesting to note that when Robert Cave sold his three hundred acres east of the Rucker property, he named it Cavesville. Of course neither plantation was a village in the modern sense of the word.

On December 3, 1864, John Christopher Durrer married Sarah Francis Rucker, and this was the connection by which Friendly Acres became Durrer property. It remains so down to the present day. Ruckersville was not a planned village, and as far as we know neither the Rucker family nor the Durrer family had much to do with the establishment of Ruckersville as a true village.

The Mitchell family seems to have included several entrepreneurs who began that work. It began with John Mitchell in 1841 when the Ruckersvile Post Office was established, and ended when W.B.F. Mitchell died in 1901. His estate included seven acres, dwelling houses, a blacksmith shop and a store. By this time there was even a race track nearby.

Ruckersville probably reached its zenith in the early 1900s as a community of well-to-do farmers. At the center of this community was a small business district almost entirely run by two brothers, Alvin and Charles Dulaney. Their efforts were undoubtedly supported by a grandfather who had profited greatly from investments in the Gulf Oil Company. The brothers started a general store in 1911. By 1914 they added an automobile agency. Of course, this led to a garage and the selling of gas. Charles was a founder of the Charlottesville Oil Corporation, a Gulf Oil agency.

Maps of the area during this general period supplied by several longtime residents show that there was a millinery shop, a wheelwright shop, a "court house," a shoemakers shop, a tannery, a distillery and a tavern.

In 1932 U.S. 29 was built through Greene County. The Dulaney Brothers Garage was removed to allow construction of the road. Charlottesville was now only sixteen miles away with automobile agencies, garages and larger general stores. The importance of Ruckersville declined, and in 1947 Alvin Dulaney sold the store building. However, in recent times Ruckersville has developed into a sort of terminus for a corridor of various kinds of stores and businesses extending north from Charlottesville. There is now more business in Ruckersville than it previously had seen, but the feeling of rural community is gone.

Stanardsville

William Stanard of Roxbury, his plantation about eleven miles south of Fredericksburg, brought his family to "Greene County." He may have moved his family to keep it from possible danger during the Revolutionary War. He returned to Spotsylvania County, and by 1794 he had decided to create a little town in his "Greene County." He had mapped

This was the store of the Dulaney Brothers. It was undoubtedly built before World War I. Today, it is still used and houses several antique dealers.

out a parcel of forty-five acres, which he called Stanards Ville, and marked ninety half-acre lots, selling a number of them himself. In that year he succeeded in having the Virginia General Assembly pass an act that created Stanardsville as an unincorporated town. It remains the only officially recognized town in Greene County.

Stanardsville was admirably chosen to meet the needs of travelers along the road (later known as the Richmond Road) over the mountains. Within a year it had a tavern. By 1798 another tavern was advertised for sale in the Richmond paper. By 1815 it was a thriving little town of one hundred and forty-two residents, five stores, two taverns, one tan yard, a saddler, one boot and shoe shop, a tailor, two blacksmiths, a wheelwright, one hatter, a gunsmith and a physician. Two or three houses remain from this early period. One of those store keepers was John Sorrille, also home secretary to President Madison.

The need for taverns and hotels was not only caused by travel along the road over the mountains but by the fact that in 1838 Stanardsville became the county seat. Stanardsville was undoubtedly chosen for the county seat because it was centrally located in the county, was the only recognized town in the county and at that time had the only post office in the county. This event caused a flurry of building, which included the courthouse, the old jail and the county clerk's office.

The Lafayette Hotel and at least eight other buildings remain from this period between 1838 and 1861.

The Lafayette Hotel was built by Robert Pritchett in 1840. It is a federal-style building, three stories in height. Its wall, three layers of brick thick, surround a large

This house was built by John Sorrille, a local storekeeper and home secretary for President Madison. *Picture by Bill Steo. Permission for use from Gary Lowe.*

central hall and stairway with rooms on either side. On the first floor there is a dining room on the left, and an ordinary on the right, though in its earliest days it may have been a "company room" where supplies were stored until the delivery company from Richmond needed them. On the second floor there is a ballroom above the ordinary. In its early days, the third floor was apparently simply an open sleeping space.

The hotel has experienced a remarkable history. It remained in the Pritchett family in parts until 1891, but it had been handled by managers for probably twenty years. Amanda Saunders managed the hotel for a time. James Saunders, as postmaster in Stanardsville from 1871 to 1880, used it as the post office, and they apparently used it as a sort of spa or retreat for people from such places as Charlottesville and Richmond. It finally took a court order for the hotel to pass into the hands of Magnolia Blakey, but she sold it a little more than two years later. During the next twenty years it changed hands five times, and at one time was considered as a possible hospital.

In 1913 the hotel was purchased by T.W. Moyers and became known as the Blue Ridge Hotel. The Moyer family, including nine boys, lived in the hotel, so there could have been little room for visitors. During this period the parts of the building were used for a post office, a telephone exchange, law offices, the Greene County Record, a watch repair shop and a solar heat salesroom. After Mr. Moyers's death in 1940 the building passed to other family members, resuming the name of Lafayette Hotel.

Finally it has returned with considerable success to its original purpose. Once more it is a bed-and-breakfast and restaurant.

The Lafayette Hotel was built c.1838. Over the years it has seen a number of uses, but currently is an upscale bed and breakfast and an equally important restaurant. *Picture by Bill Steo. Permission for use from Alan Pyles.*

Stanardsville must have suffered through the post-Civil War period along with the whole South. The next period of building had to wait until a twenty year period at the turn of the century, and a number of Victorian houses remain in a village waiting to welcome visitors to a recognized historic area.

Quinque

The Quinque Post Office was established in 1886 several miles west of Ruckersville on what is now U.S. 33. Mary E. Stephens was the first postmistress. It might well be said that for many years the Stephens family owned Quinque. At one time Quinque consisted of a store, a blacksmith shop, a wheelwright shop, a distillery and a mill. There is one belief that Quinque was named for the five buildings that existed there at that time.

Today Quinque consists of a grocery store, the former mill (now a farm implement store), the Ryan Funeral Home (containing the post office) and two houses. The final member of the Stephens family to own the Stephens House passed away only several years ago and the Stephens house may soon become a bed-and-breakfast.

This house built c.1850 was the mansion of the Stephens family, owners of Quinque for years. *Picture by Bill Steo. Permission for use of picture from Reynold Harbison.*

Celt

Celt extended for a couple of miles along what has become known as Celt Road, once the road from Stanardsville to Charlottesville. Its center was probably a house purchased by John I. Baugher, and where he was postmaster of Celt from 1909 until 1934. He probably had a small store there as well. Across the road was a schoolhouse. There is some reason to believe that this was a school for black children. About a mile north, on the west side of the road, is the C.R. Chapman Store. The store sits on the site of the Old Pine Grove School, and it seems possible that the store building is simply a renovation of the school building. Several years ago Mr. Chapman was killed during an attempted robbery, and since that time the store has been empty. About half a mile south of the former post office is a small concrete block house now renovated beyond recognition. It was Abe Dulaney's small store in the early 1940s.

Amicus

William Chapman probably built a store here before 1886. It was located on Celt road about a mile north of the C.R. Chapman Store, which marked the northern end of the hamlet of Celt. He established a post office at the store in 1887. Since the Chapman family owned at least three of the corners of that intersection, one might wonder that it was not called Chapman Corners. However, the Chapmans went so far as to name their home Amity. It seems that at least one person in the family knew some Latin, and appreciated the fact that this word had its root in the Latin verb "to love." Amicus was a good name.

The store continued until about 1920, and then stood empty for many years until the Seventh Day Adventist Church used it for their place of worship. When it was no longer big enough for their congregation they moved to Ruckersville. It was taken over by a small Baptist group.

A small building still standing across the road was for years used by the voters of the Monroe District of Greene County, and helps us to understand the importance of this corner.

Roudabush

North and on the west side of Celt road, on the north bank of Swift Run River, was Roudabush. One is tempted to call this place Beazley, for it was Beazley land for many years. As early as 1855 there is a deed, which located a sawmill, a gristmill, a house in which a cooper lived and a storehouse in the area. In 1895 Z.S. Roudabush bought two and a half acres of this land. It included the Merchant Oakland Mill (sawmill), a gristmill and the miller's house. Zachariah Roudabush established a post office (an existing photograph suggests that the post office was part of the gristmill), which continued from 1898 until 1915. The gristmill, and presumably the post office,

The C.R. Chapman store in Celt, Virginia. It was open until about 2000 when Mr. Chapman was killed in an attempted robbery. *Permission to use picture from Kenneth Chapman.*

burned at about this time, and Roudabush sold the remaining property in 1916. A store building, which may be the original Beazley storehouse, now sits near the site of the mills and the miller's house.

The Corner Store

While most hamlets grew up in the late 1800s or early 1900s, the Corner Store is a sort of latter-day village. Originally it was only a store and service station, and it is safe to say that it would never have developed if U.S. 29 had not been built in 1932. Lawrence Bishop built the store in 1936 at an intersection about three miles south of Ruckersville. Shortly afterward, Sterling Lamm built a store, service station and four tourist cabins across the road and to the south.

In 1996 the corner was leased to the Sheetz Company, which built a modern convenience store and service station. The original Corner Store building was moved a short distance north and became a nursery business.

At the same time a shopping mall was developed on the other side of U.S. 29. The mall now contains a grocery store, a restaurant, a bank, a video rental, a dry cleaner and several other stores. While the original stores were slanted toward travelers who needed gasoline, or even a place to stay overnight, the stores now serve the many residents who live in various subdivisions: Rolling Hills, Wetsel Village and Preddy's Creek.

Erald

Erald (or Earald according to some) Post Office was located near the entrance to the old Thornton place, mentioned earlier in the "Early Roads" section, near the confluence of the Conway and South Rivers. Jackson Lafayette Thornton was postmaster in the early years of the post office, which existed from 1894 until 1924. The post office was located in a store building, possibly a former slave house. Howell Haney was the storekeeper.

It seems likely that two mills were the first evidence of business in the area of Erald. The Miller Mill was a gristmill known to have two earlier owners, and dating well back in the 1800s. A second mill was also near the South River. A sawmill was located just south of the State Road 619 (Dundee Road) bridge across South River. Its considerable age is indicated by the fact that it was a water-powered, pit sawmill.

The Dundee School, a public school from 1896 to 1925, was located about one mile west of the post office. In 1854 Anthony Thornton sold one acre of land to the trustees of the Dundee Baptist Church. It continued on that site until 1929 when it relocated, and was instrumental in forming the Stanardsville Baptist Church. Across the road from the post office George Haney had his blacksmith shop.

Dawsonville

Dawsonville was located on the Fredericksburg Road about two miles east of U.S. 29. Post office records date back to 1852 when John G. Herndon was postmaster, but there is reason to believe that the hamlet developed some time before that date. Of course, Mr. Herndon also had a store. It is said that the post office moved back and forth across the road as opposing national political parties came into power.

The Orange Mills (sawmill and gristmill) may have been the first business at Dawsonville. The hamlet came to include a blacksmith shop, the Dawsonville School and a shoe shop. Today only a large brick house and an old store building remain to remind us of Dawsonville.

Borneo

Today the site for Borneo does not seem a likely location for a post office, a mill and a store. When Edward W. May purchased this land along Welshman Run in 1882, there was a road connecting it with Celt Road. At this time the Celt hamlet did not exist, and Borneo was a convenient place to go to the mill, buy a few groceries and get mail. The road through Borneo was a favored road for travel along the southern part of Greene County and through Simmons Gap. In 1908 Mr. May sold all his holdings, and the deed made arrangements for his care in his final days or years. This was just about the time that the hamlet of Celt came into existence. Now Borneo is a quiet little space along the Welshman Run where one can sit and wonder how it got its name.

Wetzel

After owning a small boat, which he used as a store, moving up and down the Mississippi River and stopping where he might sell his goods, John Wetsel returned to Greene County in 1860 where he farmed and set up a store. At the time it was in an ideal place for a store. It was about four miles from Ruckersville, and about a mile from the present location of the Corner Store, which did not exist at that time. It was on the well-traveled road that led through Borneo at a later date. He established a post office in 1885, which following his death in 1895, his wife continued until 1908. Now the entrance to the Rolling Hills subdivision is about where the store once stood.

14

THE SHENANDOAH NATIONAL PARK

Any history of the Shenandoah National Park involves eight Virginia counties, a scenic road one hundred and five miles long (Skyline Drive), the introduction of the Civilian Conservation Corps into the park, the forming of an unusual number of local, state and federal committees and commissions, both state and federal legislation and the relocation of a large number of people. Greene County was a part of much of this action.

One might reasonably say that the first intimation of a park came in 1894 when George Pollock inherited five thousand acres of land in the Blue Ridge, southeast of Luray, Virginia. There he developed the Skyland Resort, and urged a number of his wealthy, influential friends in the Washington, D.C., area to come and enjoy the locale. When the National Park Service, founded in 1916, began considering the possibility of a national park in the eastern states, several of these friends began to tout the Skyland area as a possibility. In 1926 a private organization, the Shenandoah National Park Association, began a fund drive. Created to buy land for the park, the fund would help convince Congress to accept the Shenandoah National Park. It was soon joined by a State Conservation and Development Commission with similar purposes. In the same year, Congress passed a bill that would create a Shenandoah National Park when titles to the land had been passed to the secretary of the interior. It was a recognized fact that the federal government had never appropriated funds for the purchase of park lands.

In 1928 the Virginia Legislature appropriated $1,000,000 for the purchase of land, but took action to reduce the proposed size of the park and thus reduce the final cost. It also passed a "blanket condemnation" act, which would presumably facilitate the acquisition of lands.

In the next several years there were a number of problems causing delays. Perhaps the greatest of these was the fact that, though owners of 141,000 acres accepted the decisions of court-appointed appraisers, one hundred and thirty owners of 19,000 acres challenged the appraisals. Then, in early 1934, about the time most of the legal battles were being solved, the National Park Service director announced that "all inhabitants of the park lands, whether landowners, tenants, or squatters," would have to leave before the federal government would accept title to the park. About six hundred families in the Blue Ridge, between three and four thousand people, would be affected. It seems likely that most of the officials involved in the formation of the park held the common opinion that mountain people were poor, ignorant and living a substandard life, which could only be improved by moving them down out of the mountains. This opinion was not held by everyone, but the ruling came at a time when there was great pressure to open the park and begin reaping the economic benefits expected from that action. The ruling should not have come as a complete surprise to Virginian authorities, but there had been a sort of understanding among some that elderly people might be able to live out their lives in the park area.

At the same time there were opposing ideas of what the park should be and do. There was a prevailing opinion in the National Park Service that the park should return to its natural state before two hundred years of human habitation. Of course, we now know that those mountains had known human habitation for thousands of years. Others thought it should show the mountaineers' way of living, but that idea also failed.

Gina Haney grew up and went to school in Greene County. Her family's long presence in Greene County surely made her feel as if this were home. Gina, with a strong academic background that includes a master's degree from the University of Michigan, wrote an article for the *Greene County Magazine*. The article is written from the view point of the Episcopal Missionary effort in the Blue Ridge Mountains. She writes the following:

> *The indigenous mountain dwellings, which these women missionaries to the upland south faced, in their minds were emblematic of a people lacking civilization. One room houses with dirt floors and without glazed windows seemed to them architectural testaments to the need for change. While mountaineers did sometimes inhabit shoddy or dilapidated dwellings, most were solidly built, wood-framed or hewn-log structures. While one room houses were common the average mountain household occupied a moderately furnished dwelling which, counting loft space above stairs, enclosed three or four rooms. Cleared and delineated by fence lines, yards surrounding these dwellings usually contained a variety of small outbuildings and root cellars (1996, 1-5).*

In the same article she quotes Florence Towle from her first year in Pocosan Hollow: "The people—well, they are just hopeless, absolutely hopeless. The church is certainly up against a tough proposition if it ever expects to do anything with them and, of course, that's what the mission is for" (1996, 1-5).

Gina continues:

> *[B]y March of 1907, one year after the Towle sisters arrived in Pocosan Hollow, they succeeded in having a shed-roofed addition built onto the south gable-end of their mission house. By partitioning this shed addition into two rooms, the Towle sisters achieved individual spaces for cooking and storing clothing (1996, 1-5).*

After three years Florence wrote about her neighbors: "They are as apt to make coffee in the tea kettle as in the coffee pot, or to make up the bread in the washbasin as in the bread pan" (Haney 1996, 1-5).

All these events occurred in the middle of the Great Depression, and during President Roosevelt's early efforts to pull the nation out of that depression. One of those efforts was of particular interest to Virginians and those concerned with developing the park. In 1935 a bill was passed, which in effect created the Civilian Conservation Corps, and eight camps were established in, or near, the park area. The earliest men in these camps were Virginians, and their work is most obvious in the quality of the stonework along the Skyline Drive.

Before the men got to their camps, most of them were sent to army camps for physical conditioning, inoculations, etc. When they got to their camps, they found that they were organized much like the army. They probably found only tents to live in, but eventually they built barracks, mess halls, kitchens and bathroom/latrines. Work was hard. They found themselves working on Skyline Drive, on eroded hillsides, on drainage ditches, in sawmills, on stonework along the drive and even as occasional park guides. They were building a national park (Eagle 1999).

There remained the problem of getting people out of the mountains. The court battles were finally won, but there were elderly people who could not move themselves. There were also those who either were tenants, or simply squatters who had nothing at all with which to relocate. This would seem to be a matter for the state to handle, but it soon became evident that it required federal assistance. Several years' delay occurred as this project was passed from government agency to government agency. Some people were placed with relatives. The Welfare Agency purchased a few homes, rented several houses and repaired and made livable some houses that families had already owned. A few mentally impaired folk were simply placed in institutions.

In Greene County, as in other counties, the Federal Farm Mortgage Corporation eventually was given the job of relocating a number of residents. Acreage was purchased, mostly from the Church of the Brethren in the Haneytown area. Against the advice of those who worked with and knew the mountain folk, a "French Village" concept was adopted. Some sort of plan was implemented to orient the people to their new life. Sixteen houses were built close together, and the men were supposed to farm the rest of the land cooperatively. It is likely that they never farmed any of the land. Some "make-work" jobs were provided, and several men apparently shared parts of a nearby farm, but not cooperatively. Chicken houses were built as another possible source of income. (There was no industry nearby to provide income.) The project was a failure. It is doubtful if much rent was ever paid, except in the form of work done for the project. None of the houses were purchased by those brought down from the mountains. By 1946 the houses were empty of occupants. The houses were cut in two and sold, and the land was sold as Federal surplus land.

Bitterness remains to this day. Many of those still living, as well as their children and relatives, resent the manner in which their land was taken from them by condemnation.

U.S. 33 running through Swift Run Gap. The Skyline Drive runs over the bridge seen in the picture.

They resent the often small amounts they were paid for their land, and the manner in which they were moved out of their homes. They resent the apparent attitude of Shenandoah Park officials that they were poor, ignorant and unable to maintain a livelihood where they were living in the mountains. In recent years they have joined in an effort to force those officials to represent them more accurately in presentations to park visitors. In addition to the feelings of those who were moved, "lowlanders" were unhappy that secondary roads over the mountains and through the park area—roads they were accustomed to using—were closed to them. Park officials began to charge admission into land for which the people of Virginia had already paid. There remains a distrust of government in general, and one may still find those who believe that the National Park Service would like to condemn more land for a larger park.

About 1990 a group of people in Greene County got together and called themselves the Children of the Shenandoah. For the most part they were children of parents who had lived up in the Blue Ridge Mountains. In fact, a number of them were old enough to remember that as children they too had lived in those mountains. They enjoyed showing pictures of those old times, but there was a much greater purpose for their meeting. In recent years they have joined in an effort to force park officials to represent them more accurately in presentations to park visitors. We have already learned about the stereotype that all residents of the mountains were poor, uneducated and rather simple people living in poor housing with little farming ability. In moving people out of the mountains someone burned a house before those who lived there were taken away. It is doubtful that this happened often, but it is a story that could easily be expanded. As a matter of fact, there were some people who lived in good housing in the mountains. Considering the record of the work of the Episcopal Missions, it is probable that a number of children had some schooling, and that their parents had had some religious training.

We have seen that there were at least two opposing views of these mountaineers. The view of the leaders of the Shenandoah National Park, and the one relayed to holiday visitors, was the poorer side. In addition the manner in which people were moved from the mountains caused anger from groups like the Children of the Shenandoah. Presumably similar groups started in all of the counties adjacent to the park. Recent information indicates that the Children of the Shenandoah have been effective. Information now given to visitors shows a considerably different, and more understanding attitude toward the mountaineers.

15

TRAVEL IN GREENE COUNTY

In Colonial Virginia the leaders were all Englishmen who followed English patterns in their government. In England the keeping of roads was consigned to parishes. In those days the church was an arm of the government, and the parish was that geographical area where a particular church had oversight. Because the colonial parishes were too large, the Colonial Virginia Assembly gave the care of roads to counties. County courts were to appoint road surveyors or supervisors for the making of new roads and the upkeep of old roads. Courts were also responsible for the selection of men who were to work or provide workers for each project. For instance, Stanardsville was founded when it was still in Orange County. A direct route to the Madison Courthouse, also still in Orange County, was needed. A survey had to be made, the Orange County Court had to select workers and early in the 1800s we find a road named Madison-Culpeper Road. Today that road is State Road 230. From that early day, the story of keeping the roads is one in which the colony or state government gradually took responsibility. Court orders show a continuing effort to require the upkeep of roads. It was when county court efforts did not prove adequate, or when there were complaints about the roads, that colonial officials would sometimes provide rulings to make the courts more effective. This was the beginning of a gradual takeover of the road system by the colony or state, a process which was not complete until modern times.

One of the greatest concerns in the early days was the need for good transportation through the Blue Ridge Mountains. One law, among a number of such laws in 1764, was passed for a road through Swift Run Gap. This road would go through present Greene County. Such a road would require a costly effort on the part of more than one county, and while the state assembly made some provision for financing it, the result was unsatisfactory. Events in the Revolutionary War as well as the French and Indian War emphasized the need for better means of communication and moving supplies across the mountains. Taking more responsibility for transportation, the state government authorized the construction of several turnpikes, including the Swift Run Gap Turnpike. It was fifty years later that the Harrisonburg-Richmond Turnpike reached Stanardsville, and a tollhouse was set up there near the John Sorrille house. The turnpike went on to Gordonsville and Richmond, but upon viewing a picture of

U.S. 33 in Ruckersville before the road was paved.

the road in Ruckersville taken in the early 1900s, one must wonder that it could have been called a turnpike.

The French and Indian War and the Revolutionary War emphasized the need to improve ways of communicating and of moving supplies. The result was an effort to improve river travel, and this included the development of canals. They accomplished little, and in any event, "Greene County" was never considered.

It was in the mid-1820s that railroads became a factor in the development of means of communications and transporting supplies through Virginia and the nation. This inspired considerable rivalry between canals, roads and railroads, but railroads never reached Greene County.

The Virginia Assembly was adamantly opposed to interference from the national government, but nevertheless the National Postal System extended a Post Road System into Virginia. In 1815 a post road from Madison, Virginia, reached Stanardsville. Another post road passed through Stanardsville in 1820, apparently using the Harrisonburg-Richmond Road. By 1840 a post road from Luray, Virginia, passed through Fletcher to Stanardsville and beyond. However poor they may have been, they were probably better than other roads in the state.

From 1784 to 1792 the Virginia Assembly issued what were essentially franchises to four or five stage companies to carry mail along established routes. The first stage line through what is now Greene County ran along the Harrisonburg-Richmond Road before the turnpike was completed. This appears to be a typical stagecoach schedule:

From Gordonsville, by Barboursville, Liberty Mills, Burtonsville, Stanardsville, Ruckersville, Barboursville, and Stony Point to Gordonsville, 58 miles, three times a week. Leave Gordonsville every Tuesday, Thursday and Saturday at 11 A.M., arrive at Stanardsville same day by 8 P.M. and at Gordonsville next day by 4 P.M.[1]

Today when we plan a trip of any distance, we hope to find a hotel, motel or bed-and-breakfast. When travelers in the earlier days of our country set out on a trip, they hoped to find a tavern at the end of the day. Like today they were found on the most used roads or in villages, and they supplied the amenities of our bed-and-breakfasts. One writer notes:

[T]averns and ordinaries themselves covered a broad spectrum from the large mansion-like buildings down to the very humblest of structures, often no more than a dozen feet square, and of the rudest log construction and finish. They sometimes appeared wonderfully rustic and picturesque to the traveler with their steep roofs, multiple porches and oddly placed additions. Inside they could be anything from delightful to disgusting in the fare and accommodation they presented to the visitor. At the meaner sort of back country one might be offered only hoecake and bacon washed down with coffee or whiskey; but at the best the food might be described in superlatives (Hewlon 1985).

As a passing observation it should be noted that George Washington traveled through "Greene County" sometime during the mid-eighteenth century. Returning from a surveying trip across the Blue Ridge Mountains, he found a tavern probably along the present State Road 609. His opinion of it was very poor. Perhaps it is just as well that we have no further information about that tavern. In 1770 May Burton was granted permission to open a tavern by the Orange County Court. When that one burned, he built another. In 1860 Robert Miller was granted permission to have a "house of entertainment" (a tavern) on what is now U.S. 33, ideally located at its intersection with the Mountain Road.

When Stanardsville was recognized as an unincorporated town by the Virginia Assembly in 1794, it immediately began to take advantage of its location on the main road in the county. In that same year Andrew Fleck applied for a license to have a tavern. In 1805 Robert Branham took out fire insurance on his tavern in the center of town. There were others as well, and when Stanardsville became the county seat of newly formed Greene County (1838), Robert Pritchett built the present-day Lafayette Hotel. Other hotels were built, and unfortunately destroyed by fires. In the twentieth century automobiles and good roads made travel over long distances possible. Hotels in small towns became less important.

---

1. This schedule was provided with the help of Ann Wynn, a former president of the Greene County Historical Society.

In recent years there has been a trend toward staying in rural places such as Stanardsville when going to a university graduation, a wedding or a visit to some nearby scenic place, and the Lafayette Hotel became a bed-and-breakfast and restaurant. Across the street is another, and there are several more in the county.

16

EDUCATION IN GREENE COUNTY

E ducation surely came to what is now Greene County with the earliest families. It was home teaching. Boys were taught by their fathers through advice, example and personal experience such things as how to handle farm animals, how to fit a field for planting and how to plant tobacco and grain. Girls were taught by their mothers such things as how to garden, how to cook and how to keep house. In most cases it was not formal, but for better or worse education happened. Children were somehow taught those skills that they would need to live and prosper as adults.

As we have seen, we find the earliest positive effort toward education in the 1769 will of William Monroe, an immigrant from England who could neither read nor write. He provided for his wife and stepdaughter. The rest of his estate was to be sold, and the money from the sale would be used to educate poor children. In that day "poor children" meant, of course, poor boys.

Apparently no action was taken on the Monroe Fund until 1811. At that time the general assembly made legislation that provided for money from the expropriated glebe lands of the Episcopal Church to be combined with the Monroe Fund. They then created the Orange County Humane Society to administer the fund. Greene County did not exist at this time, but when it was formed in 1838 it asked for its share of the fund. John Pendleton, a member of Orange County Humane Society, presumably sometime between 1811 and 1838 wrote, "We commenced with a capital of some $13,000; we educated over a thousand children and increased the capital to about $30,000" (Scott 1907, 142). Pendleton was making an objection to Greene County sharing the Monroe Fund. Perhaps we cannot contradict his statement, but we may wonder how the society managed to educate a thousand poor children and more than double the fund when there were no public schools. At that time Greene County did receive $5,000. In 1858 the general assembly created the Greene County Humane Society to administer the county's share of the Monroe Fund, but the account was not settled until after the Civil War when the county received the remainder of its share—a total of about $10,000. Of course there were still no public schools, and we do not know what efforts were made to implement the wishes of Monroe's will. The society proceeded to invest the money in a number of personal loans. It is interesting to note that Orange County invested its share of the fund in Confederate bonds, which by the end of the Civil War had no value.

In 1870 public schools were established in Virginia. At that time, the Greene County Humane Society obtained the help of the courts to reinterpret the will. Instead of attempting to help individual poor children, the society contributed money to lengthen the school year by a month. In subsequent years the interest was used to help meet the cost of new buildings. In recent years the society has come to doubt the wisdom of making personal loans, and is now investing in certificates of deposit. Currently the society is contributing $1,500 yearly to the school budget from a fund of about $50,000.

School buildings did not come early to Greene County. However, it must have been in the early years of the nineteenth century when neighboring families joined forces to provide more formal training for their children by hiring a teacher. This happened in the South River area. Several families worked together, and a small school was built on the Shelton farm, not far from the corner of the South River Road and the Octonia Road. In recent years the building still existed, but was being used as a sort of toolshed. The Powell School, also an "old field" school, may still be seen on the Carol Dean land along State Road 810. Such schools were called "old field" schools because they were often placed in a field where fertility had been reduced by overuse.

Apparently in a number of cases, well-to-do families simply hired a teacher on their own. In the 1850 census of Greene County, Albert Hudson is listed as part of the George W. Price family along with two sons. His occupation is given as "schoolmaster." This practice continued into the early 1900s even though public schools were available at that time. Miss Senannie Beaty is quoted as saying, "[O]f our kinfolks and people we knew best everybody, it was the Dulaneys, the Earlys, the Freys, Chapmans, Stephens, all those had teachers in their homes for their children."[1] Since Miss Beaty was born in 1892, she was probably remembering the very early 1900s. In those years, Senator Nathaniel B. Early went so far as to have a small schoolhouse built, primarily for his own children.

There were also private schools. At one time Guildford Hall was Guildford Academy for Girls where Dr. John Early's family took in girls to board and instruct them. We have a monthly report form of the Greene Classical and Mathematical Academy, Stanardsville, Virginia, for the year 1857–1858, F.M. McMullen, principal. A letter to the editor published in the *Greene County Record* of January 28, 1926, which describes Stanardsville in 1868, tells us that in that year there was a "schoolhouse upstairs" in a house near the center of the village. Quite likely this was the McMullen School. In that same year Francis M. McMullen bought nine and three-quarters acres along what is now 215 Madison Road, and established Forest Hill Academy. The building is still there. By 1876 the Stanardsville District School trustees began to use it as a public school. This continued at least until 1903 when McMullen sold the property,

---

1. From a conversation with Miss Senannie Beaty taped March 1979 by Esther G. Davis, a charter member of the Greene County Historical Society.

The Powell "Old School." *Shown with permission of Carol and Ellen Deane.*

and the Trustees purchased land on the north side of U.S. 33 and in the eastern part of Stanardsville for an elementary school. There surely were other schools at that time as well.

When public schools were established in Virginia in 1870, county officials appointed a committee to divide the county into three districts. The boundaries may have changed somewhat but the names of the districts remain: Monroe, Ruckersville and Stanardsville. There was a County School Board at this time, but its primary duty seems to have been the establishing of a school budget. District School trustees were given the duty of providing schools and teachers. Land and buildings seem to have been provided over a number of years as the need became obvious. School records listed schools by number, but many were known by the name of the community or road where they were located. Unfortunately it is difficult—perhaps impossible—to correlate all the names and numbers. However, in 1921–22 each district seems to have had eight white schools and two or three black schools. It is an unfortunate fact that black high school students were taken to the Burley School in Charlottesville until integration became the rule in 1956.

In most cases the early schools were of log construction and contained one room, eighteen by twenty feet in size, with two windows. School property included one stove, one axe, one bucket and one dipper. However, several pictures of schools seem to show schools that were frame structures with more windows. By our standards, all would have been inadequate.

Grade school constructed in 1915 by Greene County School Board.

Orthography (this may have meant spelling in that day), reading, writing, arithmetic, grammar and geography were to be taught in all schools. United States and Virginia history might be taught in the higher grades if they did not interfere with the more important subjects. It seems that those who controlled the subjects to be taught had not strayed far from the early parents' concern to teach their children those things they would need for adult living.

In 1912 one teacher agreed to teach for three or more months at $15.00 a month. Since this contract began on January 4, 1912, we can assume that the school year actually started two or three months earlier. In 1947 the average annual salary for elementary teachers was $1,343.15, while for high school teachers the average annual salary was $1,629.78. What a great difference that is from salaries today.

In 1922 a gradual process of consolidation began when the work of school trustees in the three districts was integrated into the county school board. Serious consolidation began with the construction in 1925 of the first William Monroe School, combining high school and elementary classes. In 1926–27 a school bus route from Ruckersville to Stanardsville was established. The first bus was a pickup truck, which reputedly had been a dogcatcher's truck. However, the lack of transportation—particularly in the mountain area—continued. For years many students walked miles to school. A few rode horses. The lack of transportation was relieved through the establishment of mission schools by the Episcopal Church and the Church of the Brethren

William Monroe High School after its most recent renovation. *Picture by Bill Steo.*

from the early 1900s until about 1934–35 when public school buses became more numerous.

By 1954 there were only two one-teacher schools: Wyatt's Mountain and High Top. By 1960 there were three consolidated elementary schools: Stanardsville, Ruckersville and Dyke, and one high school. In March of 1963 the new, modern William Monroe High School was dedicated. In 1976 the Greene County Primary School was built, replacing the three former elementary schools. Various vocational courses were added to the school curriculum beginning in 1976, and for a time the former Dyke Elementary School became the County Alternative Learning Center. In 1985 these courses were housed in the new Greene County Technical Center. Since then, with the rapid increase in population in Greene County, it has been necessary to add other buildings: Nathanael Greene Elementary School (1979) and Ruckersville Elementary School (1997) have been added, and the continued growth in Greene County population has brought the realization that more school building may soon be necessary.

In more recent times there has been a growing discontent with the public school system through the country, and Greene County was no exception. One of the reasons for the widespread discontent was the Supreme Court decision that there could be no prayers in public schools. This has somehow led to the belief that the schools are not only neutral concerning religion, but are actually anti-religious. Widely publicized violence in the schools has lead to a concern for the safety of children in school. There has developed a persistent belief on the part of some people that standards of learning have been lowered.

One answer to these concerns is the growth of Christian schools. In Greene County the Bible Baptist Church founded the United Christian Academy in 1979. It now has over two hundred students from preschool to twelfth grade. Its continued growth indicates that for a number of parents this is a solution to today's school problems.

Another effort to give children a better education is home schooling. This is not like the early teaching of those skills needed for children to survive as adults. The current effort has a support group, which provides various kinds of help, and it attempts to give children the same courses available in the public school in a more favorable environment. This effort is being used in Greene County.

17.

GREENE COUNTY IN THE TWENTIETH CENTURY

Though we have carried the separate history of both the mountain area and the eastern section of Greene County into the twentieth century, at some indefinable point the history of both becomes one.

The dominant feature of the twentieth century was war. Between 1917 and 2007 the United States has been involved in six wars. This does not include several instances when military action was taken, but was not called war. Small as it is, Greene County has participated in these wars.

Greene County newspapers for the period of World War I are missing. Participants in that war are extremely few and quite aged. If other records are correct, thirty-six men entered military service from Greene County during this war, and three were killed in action. We do know that the Red Cross undertook its usual efforts in times of human or natural tragedy. A group of Red Cross workers centered in Dyke made a name quilt. Money paid by a number of people to have their names sewn on the quilt was used for the war effort. This quilt may be seen in the Greene County Historical Museum.

As war clouds formed before World War II we can trace the change of attitude—probably throughout the whole county—in the *Greene County Record*. In October 1938 the paper published a letter to the editor by Mrs. J.E. Parrott, a feature which continued for four weeks. The letter reported in detail the political problems in Europe. The paper expressed no opinion, but one suspects that the report may have been requested by the editor. In April 1938, the paper began to side against Hitler. In May 1938 an editorial stated that the United States should send materials to the Allies, but should send no troops. On September 7, 1939, a banner headline announced the beginning of World War II, and a brief résumé of the fighting began to appear in the paper. In May 1941 a monthly list of draftees began to appear. There was an article about the Red Cross sending clothing for overseas use.

In June 1941 the county set up a plane spotters organization. Spotters were given training in the identification of planes and given duty shifts of two, three or four hours. There was a defense mass meeting, and farmers were urged to increase production of food.

After the United States was brought into the war by the actions of Japan, efforts increased. The paper began devoting nearly half of the front page to war news. There was a "victory pledge canvas," a USO drive and a scrap drive to sell war bonds. The Red Cross increased its efforts. Everyone was encouraged to start a victory garden. Along with the rest of the country, Greene County residents received ration stamps for food, gasoline and clothing to effect conservation of such staples. Women began to take wartime jobs. Five hundred and forty-four men were inducted into military service, and ten were killed in action.

During World War II the Allies made the decision, which was implemented after the war, that Korea should become independent after years of being under Japanese control. Unfortunately for the Korean people and for many nations of the world, in freedom the country was divided into two parts. North Korea fell under the influence of communist China and Russia, and South Korea was supported by democratic countries. In 1950 North Korean forces invaded the south in an effort to unite the nation under communistic rule. On June 27, 1950, the United Nations urged member nations to join in a "police action" against North Korea, and the United States joined the fight. According to the *Greene County Record*, in August 1950 the Greene County Draft Board announced pre-induction examinations. Though this action was obviously taken because of the Korean War, the newspaper made no mention of this fact. In April 1951 Virginia Governor Battle requested the aid of the Red Cross in raising money necessary to help soldiers in the Korean conflict. The Greene County Red Cross responded by conducting a drive for funds. In May of the same year the county was organized for civilian defense. The main concern seems to have been protection from atomic bombs. Later in May the *Record* announced the sale of defense bonds. Another sale of defense bonds occurred in 1953. The *Greene County Record* occasionally included notes about soldiers, but not one word about the progress of the war in Korea. Certainly some county residents were interested in current action in the war, but if so, they got it from sources outside the county. The Allied forces succeeded in driving the North Koreans back into their own territory, but for political reasons, they hesitated to do more. As a result the situation became a stalemate. President Eisenhower declared a truce in 1953; but to this day the Koreans are theoretically at war. Thirty-eight men for Greene County participated in this conflict. Two were killed in action.

Vietnam had been a colony of the French since 1867 when the Japanese conquered the country during World War II. In 1945 Vietnam was returned to the French. In 1946 Ho Chi Minh, seeking freedom for the country, led the Viet Minh in an attack against the French. The United States, trying to aid the embattled French, sent economic and military aid. This was a first step down a slippery slope. Residents of Greene County certainly knew about the war. They had news through radio and television, but the *Greene County Record* gave them very little news. In 1954 the French surrendered and the Geneva Accord divided Vietnam into North and South along the 17th parallel. When the North Vietnamese allegedly attacked the United States in the Gulf of Tonkin in 1964, real conflict broke out. In 1968 the North Vietnamese launched the Tet Offensive and, if not successful on the battlefield, they were successful in turning many Americans against the war.

In November and December 1970 an article and an editorial expressed concern over 1,600 prisoners of war. In April 1971 an article defended Lieutenant William Calley, who was instrumental in wiping out a village of innocent Vietnamese, and a note the following week indicated that the editorial had only two unfavorable responses from readers. Week by week there were announcements of men entering the military services and being moved from place to place, but there was no record of bond sales, rationing or Red Cross efforts. There was no word of battles won or lost. In 1972 the last American troops left Vietnam. The United States had lost a war, and of the forty-six men sent into service during this war one man was killed in battle.

Currently the United States is involved in a war in Iraq. Well over 3,500 of our soldiers have been killed. Since our country is still involved in this conflict, it is scarcely a time to consider how it has, or is, influencing Greene County.

If war was the dominant feature of the twentieth century, there were still a number of other events of interest during that time. The twentieth century was a time of great change. Telephones first came to Greene County when two companies (the Greene County Register and Eddins & Co.) received service in 1903. The first newspaper was published in Greene County, also in 1903. In 1914 the Dulaney Brothers of Ruckersville sold four cars. The first radio was heard in Stanardsville. In 1928 electricity came to William Monroe High School. The Virginia Department of Transportation took over the roads of Greene County in the late 1920s. U.S. 33 was paved in 1931, and U.S. 29 was built through Greene County in 1932. The Shenandoah National Park opened three years later. All was not war.

18.

The History of Greene County Government

In Colonial times the government kept a firm hand on all important county offices. The county court consisted of a number of justices of the peace, appointed by the colonial government. It met every month and tried all civil and criminal cases, except those which might require extreme punishment for white people.

The sheriff was the most powerful man in the county. He collected taxes, enforced the law and was custodian of the prisoners.

The clerk of court kept the court minutes and recorded wills, deeds and other official papers.

The crown attorney, or king's attorney, was the same as today's prosecuting attorney.

The constable was appointed by the county court. It also appointed the county coroner, who did not need to be a physician, and the county surveyor, whose most important duty seems to have consisted in maintaining the roads.

After the Revolutionary War, apparently the best course of action—perhaps the easiest course—was to follow what was already in existence. There might have been minor changes, but the state governor now made the most obvious county appointments. In 1838 the county court was composed of sixteen justices of the peace, appointed by the state governor. This court met for two purposes, separating civil cases from criminal cases. For these purposes they met on separate days. The Circuit Superior Court of Law and Chancery served a district that included both Greene and Orange Counties. This combination was also a senatorial district and elected one senator and one delegate.

Immediately after the Civil War all Southern states were under the control of the Union Army. By 1870 Virginia had written and ratified a new constitution by which the United States Congress could pass a resolution authorizing Virginia to be represented in Congress.

According to the new constitution each county continued to elect a sheriff, a commonwealth attorney, a county clerk, a county treasurer, a superintendent of the poor and a school trustee. Judges were appointed by the general assembly, and for some reason the governor now appointed a coroner. It also established a uniform system of free public schools throughout the state. White children between the ages of six and twenty-one might attend school.

In 1871 the Greene County Board of Supervisors met for the first time. In those early days the duties of the supervisors included authorizing the payment of jury members

The Greene County Courthouse. *Picture by Bill Steo.*

The old jail, originally constructed ca.1838. *Picture by Bill Steo.*

and various county employees. It also included such major projects as the building of a privy on Courthouse Square.

Times have changed, and Greene County has seen changes normal to all county governments. Greene County elects five county supervisors, who hire a county administrator, a county attorney, a county engineer, a planning director, a building inspector, a zoning inspector, a dog warden, an animal shelter manager, a waste manager to direct the work of several people in the landfill operation and a recreation director. In addition, they seek the help of a Planning Commission, an Industrial Development Authority and a Board of Zoning Appeals. These later groups are essentially unpaid volunteers. A coroner, who at one time was important enough to be appointed by the governor, no longer exists. Apparently there is a pool of doctors in the region, one of whom may be called when needed.

The county also elects a sheriff (and he in turn hires a lieutenant and about eighteen deputies), a commonwealth attorney, a county treasurer, a county clerk, a commissioner of revenue and a school board.

A number of district or regional agencies function in Greene County. These are often mandated by the federal or state government, and though they generally have federal or state funding, the county often offers some support. Though they may vary from time to time, they are:

1. The Department of Social Services, which is concerned with various types of mental health or abuse cases.

2. The Health Department, which is concerned with the physical needs of the underprivileged. It also keeps vital records of birth and death and is in charge of septic and well inspection.

3. The Jefferson Area Board of Aging, which is concerned with the many needs of the elderly.

4. The Jefferson Madison Regional Library

5. The Rapidan Service Authority, which provides water and sewage service for parts of Greene County.

6. The Region Ten Services Board, which provides for the Head Start program and assists people in various financial cases.

7. The Virginia Transit Service, which offers transportation to residents within the county and to Charlottesville.

8. The Virginia Cooperative Extension, which offers services for the rural population of the county.

There is now a circuit court to deal with both civil and criminal cases, and a juvenile and general district court, which has at various times been supported by the state or the county. This court deals with children's matters and various family matters.

19.

THE FUTURE OF GREENE COUNTY

In a number of respects Greene County development in the twentieth century has been quite typical. There were probably a number of counties in Virginia that received their first telephone service early in the century, saw their first newspaper published at about the same time, had a local bank established, saw their first cars, heard their first radio and received, in a limited way, water and sewage service. U.S. 33 was paved through a number of counties, and U.S. 29, running north and south, was built through other counties. We know that eight counties were affected by the Shenandoah National Park. Greene County was quite typical in its experience of most of these events.

In fact, the problems caused by rapid growth in the population during the past twenty-five years are what other counties also experienced. During the 1960s the Board of Supervisors, apparently believing that growth and perhaps the consequent increase in property tax income might be good for the county, relaxed the related zoning laws. This, too, may have been a typical procedure for that time. In any event, they could not have imagined the problems that rapid growth would cause later in the century.

Since 1980 the population of Greene County grew from 7,625 to 15,244 in 2000. This means that growth was virtually doubled. And if we consider the average of 2.71 residents per household, approximately 2,800 houses were built in this period.

In the past four years one may estimate that the county has approved developer requests to build approximately three thousand more homes. While that many new homes probably have not been built, one knows that there has been continued growth. However, these homes, unless they have an assessed value of $425,000 or above, do not generate enough taxes to pay for their servicing.

The rapid growth of the student population, and the consequent need for additional school buildings, has caused the school budget to rise drastically. In the year 1999–2000 there were 2,572 students, costing the county $21,027,856 or $8,175 per student. Four years later there were 2,699 students, costing the county $24,924,594 or $9,336 per student.

The need for another new building in the near future seems inevitable. The new high school–middle school expansion, completed in 2006, will cost approximately $9 million.

The need for additional funds has sometimes caused heated discussion between the Greene County School Board and the Board of Supervisors.

Recognizing the difficulty in attracting businesses without having adequate services, the county extended the sewage line from Stanardsville to Ruckersville in 1998. (Currently Ruckersville along the U.S. 29 corridor is the area of the county that businesses usually consider.) It was immediately obvious that this effort was inadequate. The new wastewater treatment plant and associated sewer lines completed in 2006 will cost another large amount, much of that to be paid by developers in Ruckersville. There is also a new water tower in Ruckersville costing somewhere near $5 million.

Ruckersville, as has been suggested, is currently the area attracting traffic-related businesses as well as various residential services. These are located along a three-mile corridor of U.S. 29, south of U.S. 33. These include: fast food restaurants, gas stations, antique shops, grocery stores, various home service stores, banks and even a motel.

Meanwhile, Stanardsville, since the completion of its bypass a few years ago, might be a quiet little town containing a courthouse, county offices, bed-and-breakfast houses and an unusual number of historic buildings. It is on the road to the Shenandoah National Park. Its only role, aside from being the site of the county government, is one of attracting tourists. Yet how these various problems are handled within this town will affect the future of this beautiful little county.

On July 16, 2007, *The Daily Progress*, a Charlottesville, Virginia newspaper, published a startling article. Wal-Mart is planning to build a supercenter just north of the intersection of U.S. 29 and U.S. 33. It will be on a sixty-eight-acre site, which will probably include other businesses. The store will employ 250 to 300 people. This may be the beginning of more development. A thirty-four-acre property north of the Wal-Mart property is being offered for sale. A fourteen-acre development about three miles south on U.S. 29 is already adding another bank to the county. The Fried Company, which has had its eye on Greene County for a number of years, is developing a sixty-five-acre property just north of the Albemarle County line.

Local people are excited but are also raising questions. Will this growth destroy the rural quality of Greene County? U.S. 29 is no more than two miles from the eastern line of the county. If growth is confined to this area, there will be plenty of rural area to the west including the mountains. Is the water system capable of supplying all this development? For a number of years the county officials have been preparing for this. Will the taxes from these developing businesses pay for an increasing need for schools, for an increased need for fire and police protection? This may well be the big question. To date, the growth in population in the county has not supported the various needs of the county.

Appendix

Greene County Statistics

Length: East to West through Stanardsville along Spotswood Trail (U.S. 33): 18 miles.

Width: North to South through Stanardsville along Madison Road (S.R. 230) and Celt Road (S.R. 622 and S.R. 604): 11 miles.

Coverage: 153 square miles; 97,920 acres.

County Seat: Stanardsville (latitude 36° 17'N, Longitude 78° 25'W).
21 miles north of Charlottesville, Virginia.
62 miles northwest of Richmond, Virginia.
76 miles southwest of Washington, D.C.

Divisions of Greene County:

	Western Piedmont Plateau	Mountainous (The Blue Ridge)
Average height above sea level	500–700 feet	3,000–3,600 feet
Average Summer temperature	75°	65°
Average winter temperature	37°	29°
Average rainfall	46 inches	51 inches
Average snowfall	23 inches	45 inches

Lakes in Greene County

Greene Mountain Lake—South of Stanardsville: 100 acres
Twin Lakes—Three lakes with a total of 770 acres
Lake Saponi—Near Albemarle/Orange County lines: 7 acres
Greene Acres Lake—north of Little Edge Mountain: 35 acres
Greene Valley Lake—north of Goodall Mountain: 15 acres

BIBLIOGRAPHY

Albemarle County Deed Books

Alexander, Edward Porter, ed. *The Journal of John Fontaine An Irish Huguenot Son in Spain and Virginia 1710–1719*. Williamsburg, VA: The Colonial Williamsburg Foundation, 1972, p. 101–109.

Allen, Rhesa M., Jr. *Geology and Mineral Resources of Greene County and Madison Counties*. Bulletin 78. Charlottesville, VA: Virginia Division of Mineral Resources, 1963.

Bean, R. Bennett. *The Peopling of Virginia*. Boston: Crescendo Publishing Co., 1938.

Beard, Charles A., and Mary R. Beard. *The Beards' New Basic History of the United States*. Garden City, NY: Doubleday and Company, Inc.

Charlottesville Daily Progress. Various issues.

Cowden, Mozel R. "What Are They Like." *Shenandoah National Journal* (1936–1937).

Cumming, William P., ed. *The Discoveries of John Lederer*. Charlottesville, VA: University of Virginia Press, 1958.

Dabney, Virginius. *Virginia the New Dominion*. Garden City, NY: Doubleday & Company, Inc., 1971.

Davison, Dexter Ralph, and Frederick W. Neve. "Mountain Mission Education in Virginia." PhD diss., University of Virginia, 1982.

Eagle, Reed L. *Everything Was Wonderful*. Shenandoah Natural History Association, Inc. 1999.

Egloff, Keith, and Deborah Woodward. *First People, the Early Indians of Virginia*. Charlottesville: The Virginia Department of Historic Resources, 1963.

Fiske, John. *Old Virginia and Her Neighbors Vol. II*. Boston: Houghton Mifflin and Company, 1879.

Greene County Record. Various issues.

Haney, Gina. "Spreading the Gospel of Domestic Order, Episcopal Missions in the Mountains of Virginia." *Greene County Magazine* 13 (1996).

Hewlon, Howard, Jr. *Backsights*. Virginia Department of Transportation, 1985.

Bibliography

Kennon, Harry G. "History of the Greene United Methodist Charge." *Greene County Magazine* 9 (1992).

Parrott, Woodie Brown. "The Formation of Greene County." *Greene County Magazine* 1 (1979): 1–10.

The Code of Virginia with the Declaration of Independence and Constitution of the United States and the Declaration of Rights and the Constitution of Virginia. Richmond, VA: William L. Richie, 1849.

Greene County Deed Books and Greene County Will Books

Greene County Deed Book 4, February 21, 1859.

Grymes, J. Randolph, Jr. *The Octonia Grant in Orange and Greene Counties.* Ruckersville, VA: Seminole Press, 1977.

Hardesty, H.H. *Hardesty's Historical and Geographical Encyclopedia (Illustrated).* Special VA edition. Richmond, Chicago and Toledo : R.A. Brock, H.H. Hardesty & Co., N.Y., 1884.

Holland, C.G., and William D. O'Ryan. "The Octonia Rock Shelter, Greene County, Virginia," *Quarterly Bulletin Archeological Society of Virginia* 18, no. 4, part 1 (June 1964).

Johnson, T.E. *A History of Greene County, Virginia.* Stanardsville, VA: Greene County Publishers, 1976.

Knight, Clyde. *Pathways to Remember.* Madison, VA: Skyline Services, Inc., 1986.

Lambert, Darwin. *The Undying Past of the Shenandoah National Park.* Boulder, CO: Roberts Rinehart, Inc., 1989.

Mansfield, James Roger. *A History of Early Spotsylvania.* Orange, VA: Greene Publishers, Inc., 1977.

Martin, Joseph. *A New and Comprehensive Gazetteer of Virginia and the District of Columbian.* Charlottesville, VA: Joseph Martin, Mosely & Thompkins, 1855.

Miller, Ann Brush. *Orange County Road Orders 1750–1800.* Charlottesville: Virginia Transportation Research Council, 1989.

Morris, Nancy, H. *Stanardsville...Then and Now.* Stanardsville, VA: Stanardsville Pride with Action, 1994.

Morrison, Samuel Eliot. *The Oxford History of the American People.* New York: The Oxford University Press, 1965.

Mumford, George W. *Third Edition of the Code of Virginia including Legislation to January, 1879.* Richmond, VA: James E. Goode, 1873.

Roberts, Graham. "The Roads of Virginia 1707–1840." PhD diss., University of Virginia, 1950.

Russelll, Patti B., ed. *Virginia United Methodist Heritage.* Bulletin of the Virginia Conference Historical Society, Vol. 25, no. 1 (Spring 1999).

Sappington, Robert E. *The Brethren in Virginia.* Harrisonburg, VA: Park View Press, 1973.

Scott, William W. *A History of Orange County, Virginia.* Richmond, VA: Waddly Co., 1907.

Steere, Edward. *The Shenandoah National Park, Its Possibility as a Historical Development* (1938), Box 1, archives, Shenandoah National Park Headquarters.

Sturgill, David A., and Mack H. Sturgill. *A History of the Sturgill Family*. Jefferson, NC: Carolina Printing and Supply Company, 1983.

Visit us at
www.historypress.net

www.ingramcontent.com/pod-product-compliance
Lightning Source LLC
Chambersburg PA
CBHW050615110426
42813CB00008B/2563